30 Rituals and Prayer Services

For Catechist and Teacher Meetings

30 Rituals & Prayer Services
for Catechist and Teacher Meetings

Alison J. Berger

TWENTY-THIRD PUBLICATIONS
185 WILLOW STREET • PO BOX 180 • MYSTIC, CT 06355
TEL: 1-800-321-0411 • FAX: 1-800-572-0788
E-MAIL: ttpubs@aol.com • www.twentythirdpublications.com

Twenty-Third Publications
A Division of Bayard
185 Willow Street
P.O. Box 180
Mystic, CT 06355
(860) 536-2611 or (800) 321-0411
www.twentythirdpublications.com
ISBN:1-58595-267-2

Library of Congress Catalog Card Number: 2003104399
Printed in the U.S.A.

Dedication

To my parents
James and Dorothy Berger
my first teachers in the faith.

Table of Contents

Introduction 1

1. Called by Name 2

2. Seek First the Kingdom of God 4

3. Prepare the Way of the Lord 6

4. Waiting with Joy 8

5. The Gifts of Advent 10

6. Celebrating the Christmas Season 12

7. We Offer Our Gifts 14

8. I Am Light—You Are Light 16

9. Presentation of the Cross 18

10. For Healing and Strength in Our Ministry 20

11. Renewing Our Baptismal Promises 22

12. Developing a Vision 24

13. Celebration of the Creed 26

14. Lord, Send Forth Your Spirit 28

15. Mary, Teacher and Disciple 30

16. Jesus, Our Master Teacher   32

17. I Am with You   34

18. Love as I Love You   36

19. Where Your Treasure Is   38

20. For Wisdom in Our Ministry   40

21. Celebrating Reconciliation   42

22. Beatitudes   44

23. Peace   46

24. The Bread of Life   48

25. We Are Called to Nurture Life   50

26. Called to Promote Justice   52

27. St. Paul, an Example of Living in Christ   54

28. Canticle of the Media   56

29. Holy Friendship   58

30. The Gift of Love   60

Introduction

"The formation [of catechists], above all, nourishes the spirituality of the catechist, so that his [or her] activity springs in truth from his own witness of life" (*General Directory for Catechesis*, #239).

30 Rituals and Prayer Services offers catechists and religion teachers the opportunity to express their faith and to bond with one another through various prayer experiences. By providing different forms of prayer it is also a source of formation in faith. These prayers aim to help catechists discover the face of God in their own lives and in the lives of those to whom they minister.

Some of the prayer services are actually rituals based on the Catholic rites found in the liturgy and the catechumenate. Others are based on seasonal customs and themes. The complete and easy-to-use prayer services and rituals involve all the participants as much as possible, often calling for spontaneous prayer and reflection as well as the prayers offered within these pages. They can be used and adapted for catechist meetings as well as retreats, days of recollection, small group meetings, and larger parish gatherings.

Lectio divina

One particular form of prayer used in this book may be less familiar to your catechists: the *lectio divina*. This is a very simple and ancient method for praying the Scriptures, both individually and as a group. If your catechists are not familiar with the lectio divina, explain the four steps before you begin.

1. The first step is to read the Scripture passage slowly, aloud or to oneself.

2. The second step is to let the words and phrases that have most touched you come to mind and heart. In a group, you are encouraged to share these.

3. The third step is to spend some silent time letting these words of Scripture lift your hearts to God.

4. The fourth step is to use the Scripture to shape your own prayer from the heart.

These 30 rituals and prayer services are only meant as a starting point. During your time of prayer together, be open to the creative action of the Holy Spirit. Allow times of silence. Adapt the prayers to your personal needs and situations. Let your prayer time together truly be a celebration of faith, hope, and love, as God guides you in your ministry in mysterious ways.

Called by Name

THEME

Our ministry as catechists is a true calling, a vocation from God and the Church.

PREPARATION

On your prayer table place a Bible (open to 1 John), a collage of photos of your catechetical team (staff, catechists, aides, and so on), and a large banner or poster that reads "I have called you by name" for the front of the prayer table. Also prepare a list of the names of your team. If possible have simple symbols for each of the names of God found in the litany. The prayer service will start out with a dialogue between the leader and the rest of the group.

GATHERING PRAYER

Leader	How many things a name can say! Who are you, my God?
All	Beloved, let us love one another, because love is from God; everyone who loves is born of God and knows God. Whoever does not love God, does not know God, for God is love. (1 John 4:7–8)
Leader	What is your name, my God?
All	"I am" that is, I am so close to you that you can count on me.... I am so close to you that you have to count on me.... I am so close to you that you can count only on me.... I am so close to you that my closeness knows no limitations of time or space.

FIRST READING	Isaiah 43:1–3, 5
Leader	I have created you, says the Lord, I have formed you, O Israel: Do not fear, for I have redeemed you; I have called you by name, you are mine.
All	I have called you by name and you are mine.
Reader One	When you pass through the waters, I will be with you; When you pass through the rivers, they shall not overwhelm you; When you walk through the fire you shall not be burned. The flame shall not consume you.
All	I have called you by name and you are mine.
Reader Two	For I am the Lord, your God, the Holy One of Israel, your Savior. Do not fear, I am with you.

LITANY OF GOD'S HOLY NAME

During the litany, the person reading the name of God, e.g., "You are our Rock," carries the appropriate symbol up to the prayer table and places it in front of the sign.

Reader Three	You are our Rock
All	Strengthen us.

Reader Four	You are our King.
All	Lead us.
Reader One	You are our Mother.
All	Save us.
Reader Two	You are our Shepherd.
All	Give us rest.
Reader Three	You are our Savior.
All	Heal us.
Reader Four	You are our Light.
All	Enlighten us.
Reader One	You are our Way.
All	Form us.
Reader Two	You are our Truth.
All	Teach us.
Reader Three	You are our Life.
All	Fill us with life.
Reader Four	You are our Love.
All	Consume us.

PRAYER OF ST. AUGUSTINE

Form two groups and have them read together the alternate verses.

Leader	How can I respond to God calling my name?
Group One	O eternal truth and true charity and dear eternity! You are my God, to you I sigh day and night. As soon as I knew you, you raised me on high so that I might see all there was to see and all that which, alone, I would never have been able to see.
Group Two	You dazzled the weakness of my vision, shining powerfully within me. Late have I loved you, O Beauty so ancient and so new, late have I loved you.
Group One	You called me, you cried out to me, you shattered my deafness. You dazzled me, you blinded me, and you finally healed my blindness.
Group Two	You breathed upon me your perfume and I breathed it and now I gasp for you. I have tasted you, and now I hunger and thirst for you. You touched me, and now I yearn for your peace.

Leader now calls the members of the team by name, one by one. As each person comes up, the leader raises his or hands over the person in prayer and says the following words: "(Name), God calls you by name. He does not say your name in vain. You answer, and your love and response are wholehearted, as is your commitment to teach God's name to the children and families you minister to." Each person then responds, "Amen."

Seek First the Kingdom of God

THEME

With this prayer ritual we can make a more formal statement of our commitment to God in our ministry.

PREPARATION

On your prayer table place a large candle, a Bible (open to Matthew 6), and handouts (preferably printed on decorated paper). On the handouts print "My Personal Covenant" and the following questions:

- Who is Jesus for me?
- Who am I and what am I called to do?
- What do I need to ask of Jesus in order to fulfill my ministry?

At the bottom of the page, write: I make a commitment to trust in you, Lord, for what I need.

GATHERING PRAYER

Leader	Loving God, you have asked us to trust in you for what we need…for our spiritual growth and for our ministry to others. Help us grow in that trust, so that you can multiply the fruit of our efforts. We ask all this in the name of Jesus your Son and our Lord.
All	Amen.

FIRST READING   1 Corinthians 1:4–9

Reader One	I give thanks to my God always for you because of the grace of God that has been given you in Christ Jesus, for in every way you have been enriched in him, in speech and knowledge of every kind—just as the testimony of Christ has been strengthened among you—so that you are not lacking in any spiritual gift as you wait for the revealing of our Lord Jesus Christ.

RESPONSORIAL PRAYER

Reader Two	For you alone, O God, my soul waits in silence; From you comes my salvation.
All	God is my salvation.
Reader Three	You alone are my rock and my salvation, My fortress; I shall never be shaken.
All	God is my salvation.
Reader Four	I trust in you, my God, at all times; I pour out my heart before you; For you, O God, are my refuge.
All	God is my salvation.

GOSPEL READING   Matthew 6:25–26, 33

Reader Five   Jesus said: "Therefore I tell you, do not worry about your life, what you will eat or what you will drink, or about your body, what you will wear. Is not life more than food, and the body more than clothing? Look at the birds of the air; they neither sow nor reap nor gather into barns, and yet your heavenly Father feeds them. Strive first for the kingdom of God and his righteousness, and all these things will be given to you as well."

All   Praise to you, Lord Jesus Christ.

THE COVENANT

Give a handout to each participant and explain that they can use it to make their own Personal Covenant to follow Christ. Allow them some quiet time to write and sign their own personal covenant with God. Play instrumental music in the background.

INTERCESSORY PRAYER

Reader One   Jesus, you told us to seek first the kingdom of God. We ask you:
- to help us grow in holiness of life;
- to increase our faith, hope, and love;
- to fill us with zeal in our ministry of the word;
- to be witnesses of your love;
- to make us persons of prayer.

Reader Two   On our part we promise to
- do our best to know and do your will;
- seek the best for the children and families in our program;
- prepare ourselves for our ministry.

Suggest that your catechists frame and keep their Personal Covenants as a reminder that Jesus is with them in their ministry.

MARY'S CANTICLE

Reader Three   My soul magnifies the Lord, and my spirit rejoices in God my savior. For he has looked with favor on the lowliness of his servant. Surely from now on all generations will call me blessed.

Reader Four   The Mighty One has done great things for me, and holy is his name. His mercy is on those who fear him from generation to generation.

Reader Five   He has shown strength with his arm; he has scattered the proud in the thoughts of their hearts. He has brought down the powerful from their thrones, and lifted up the lowly.

Reader One   He has filled the hungry with good things, and sent the rich away empty. He has helped his servant Israel remembering his mercy.

Reader Two   According to the promise he made to our ancestors, to Abraham and to his descendants forever.

All   Glory to the Father and to the Son and to the Holy Spirit, as it was in the beginning, is now, and will be forever. Amen.

Prepare the Way of the Lord

THEME

Let John the Baptist and the prophet Isaiah be our spiritual models during Advent.

PREPARATION

You will need a table with a candle with small pieces of evergreen around it (one for each participant); a bowl of water; copies of the words for "O Come, O Come, Emmanuel." Provide copies of the Bible for the readers. You might want to quickly review with participants how to respond when you call each person by name (see below). Play reflective instrumental music.

ENTHRONEMENT OF THE BIBLE

Have a simple procession into the meeting space. One reader can carry the Bible, another can carry a list of the names of your catechists and other volunteers present; each will then place what they are carrying in the appropriate place on the prayer table. Light the candle and darken the room.

GATHERING PRAYER

Leader	God of wisdom and love, we long for your presence. Help us to find you in word and sacrament, to recognize you in our personal stories and in those whom we teach. We ask this in Jesus' name.
All	Amen.

FIRST READING	Isaiah 40:1–5
Reader One	Comfort, O comfort, my people, says your God. Speak tenderly to Jerusalem, and cry to her that she has served her term, that her penalty is paid, that she has received from the Lord's hands double for all her sins. A voice cries out: "In the wilderness prepare the way of the Lord, make straight in the desert a highway for our God. Every valley shall be filled up, and every mountain and hill shall be made low; the uneven ground shall become level, and the rough places a plain. Then the glory of the Lord shall be revealed, and all peoples shall see it together, for the mouth of the Lord has spoken."

Allow a few minutes of silence. Sing or recite the refrain and two verses of "O Come, O Come, Emmanuel."

GOSPEL READING	Luke 3:15–16
Reader Two	As the people were filled with expectation, and all were questioning in their hearts concerning John, whether he might be the Messiah, John answered all of them by saying, "I baptize you with water; but one who is more powerful than I is coming; I am not worthy to untie the thong of his sandals. He will baptize you with the Holy Spirit and fire."

Again allow a few minutes of silence. Sing or recite the refrain and two more verses of "O Come, O Come, Emmanuel."

Reader Three	Lord, like Isaiah and John the Baptist, we have been called by you to be prophets, each in our own way—to prepare your way in our own lives and in the lives of the children we teach and of their families.
All	Lord, you have called me.

Turn on the lights.

Leader	God has called us each by name to this catechetical ministry. As I read your name, you are invited to affirm the renewal of your commitment by responding: Here I am, Lord, send me.

Read each name and pause for the response.

RESPONSORIAL PRAYER

Reader One	We give you thanks, O Lord, for you are good.
All	For your steadfast love endures forever.
Reader Two	We give you thanks, O God of gods.
All	For your steadfast love endures forever.
Reader Three	We give you thanks, O God of heaven.
All	For your steadfast love endures forever.

Pray together the Canticle of Simeon (Luke 2:29–32):

All	Master, now you are dismissing your servant in peace, according to your word; for my eyes have seen your salvation, which you have prepared in the sight of all the people, a light for revelation to the Gentiles, and for glory to your people Israel.

Conclude with this blessing:

Leader	This evergreen is a symbol of God's faithfulness and of our faith and hope in God. Lord bless us all, our children and our whole parish family, and bring us closer to you during this Advent season.
All	Amen.
Leader	Lord, bless our personal stories.
All	Amen.
Leader	Lord, bless us and our catechetical ministry.
All	Amen.

Leader *(dipping a piece of evergreen in the bowl of water and sprinkling the participants):*	In the name of the Father and of the Son and of the Holy Spirit.
All	Amen.

Invite the participants to take a piece of evergreen with them as a reminder of their vocation to the catechetical ministry and of the grace that God offers them in order to fulfill it.

Waiting with Joy

THEME

This Advent prayer service focuses on the ancient O antiphons.

PREPARATION

Prepare a table with the Bible (open to Isaiah 35) and an Advent wreath. You can make an Advent wreath by tying pieces of evergreen to a circle of wire. Place four candlesticks inside the wreath, with three purple candles and one pink one. **Optional:** Write out the O Antiphons on index cards, one for each participant. Decorate each card with an appropriate symbol.

GATHERING PRAYER

Leader	Everlasting God, we your people long for the coming of your Son into our world and into our hearts. Comfort us with your word and your grace. Prepare our hearts so your glory may be revealed in us and in all whose lives we touch. We ask this through Jesus your Son.
All	Amen.

FIRST READING	Isaiah 35:1–10
Reader One	O God, at your coming, the wilderness and the dry land shall be glad, The desert shall rejoice and blossom; Like the crocus it shall blossom abundantly, and rejoice with joy and singing.
All	You, our God, will come to save us.
Reader Two	We shall see the glory of Lebanon, The majesty of Carmel and Sharon, We shall see your glory, O Lord, Your majesty, O God.
All	You, our God, will come to save us.
Reader Three	The people you ransomed will return, O Lord, And come to Zion with singing; Everlasting joy shall be upon our heads, You shall bring us joy and gladness, And sorrow and sighing shall flee away.
All	You, our God, will come to save us.

GOSPEL READING   Luke 1:67–79

Zechariah was filled with joy at the vision of the coming Messiah. The O antiphons actually echo many of the images from this canticle.

Reader Four	John's father Zechariah was filled with the Holy Spirit and spoke this prophecy: Blessed are you, Lord God of Israel, for you have looked favorably on your people and redeemed us. You have raised up a mighty savior for us in the house of your servant David, as you spoke through the mouth of your holy prophets from of old, that we would be saved from the hands of our enemies and from the hand of all who hate us. Thus you have shown the mercy promised to our ancestors, and have remembered your holy covenant, the oath that you swore to our ancestor Abraham, to grant us that we, being rescued from the hands of our enemies, might serve you without fear, in holiness and righteousness before you all our days. By your tender mercy, O God, the dawn from on high will break upon us, to give light to those who sit in darkness and in the shadow of death, to guide our feet into the way of peace.

THE O ANTIPHONS

Light a candle on the Advent wreath as you pray each of the first four antiphons.

Reader One	Come, O Wisdom, you who guide all creation with your powerful, loving care,
All	Show us the way to salvation.
Reader Two	Come, O Leader of ancient Israel, you appeared to Moses in the burning bush and gave him the law,
All	Set us free with your mighty hand.
Reader Three	Come, O root of Jesse, you who have been set up as a sign for us; the nations adore you,
All	Do not delay.
Reader Four	Come, O key of David, you who open the gates of heaven,
All	Come, shatter the prison of darkness and death, and set us free.
Reader One	Come, O dawn from on high, sun of justice,
All	Shine on those who dwell in darkness.
Reader Two	Come, O king of all the nations, you who are our joy,
All	Come and save us whom you have made in your image.
Reader Three	Come, Emmanuel, our ruler, desire of the nations, our Savior,
All	Come and set us free.

CLOSING PRAYER

Leader	Loving God, let your light come to take away the darkness. Help us who await the coming of your Son Jesus to always live as children of the light. We ask this in Jesus' name.
All	Amen.

Give each participant one of the O Antiphon cards as a reminder of the spirit of Advent.

The Gifts of Advent

THEME

Together with Mary we thank God for the spiritual gifts of Advent.

PREPARATION

Prepare your prayer table with a Bible (open to Luke 1) and the Advent wreath (or a large Advent candle), leaving space for the participants to place their gifts (use a second table if necessary). Assign readers for the first reading, the introduction to Mary's Canticle, and for each verse of the Canticle. Provide construction paper, scissors, magazine pictures, glue, markers, and modeling clay (such as Sculpey). Explain at the beginning that, after the first reading, you will ask the participants to draw, do cutouts, or model a symbol or picture that represents a spiritual gift of Advent (prayer, patience, simplicity, love, compassion, repentance, expectation). Ask them to choose their material before the service begins.

GATHERING PRAYER

Leader	Loving God of all creation, we await the coming of your Son Jesus with eager longing. Let the dew of your grace rain on our hearts and bring forth gifts of patience, love, and prayer. We ask this in Jesus' name.
All	Amen.

FIRST READING Isaiah 61:1–3, 10–11

Reader One	O Lord God, your Spirit is upon me, because you have anointed me; you have sent me to bring good news to the oppressed, to bind up the brokenhearted, to proclaim liberty to the captives, and release to the prisoners.
All	Your Spirit, Lord, is upon me.
Reader Two	You send me to proclaim the year of your favor, and the day of your vengeance; to comfort all who mourn.
All	Your Spirit, Lord, is upon me.
Reader Three	You have sent me to provide for those who mourn in Zion—to give them a garland instead of ashes, the oil of gladness instead of mourning, the mantle of praise instead of a faint spirit.
All	Your Spirit, Lord, is upon me.
Reader Four	For as the earth brings forth its shoots, and as a garden causes what is in it to spring up, so you, Lord God, will cause righteousness and praise to spring up before all the nations.
All	Your Spirit, Lord, is upon me.

GOSPEL READING Luke 2:8–16

Reader Five	In that region there were shepherds living in the fields, keeping watch over their flock by night. Then an angel of the Lord stood before them, and the glory of the Lord shone around them, and they were terrified. But the angel said to them, "Do not be afraid; for see, I am bringing you good news of great joy for all the people; to you is born this day in the city of David a Savior, who is the Messiah, the Lord. This will be a sign for you: you will find a child wrapped in bands of cloth and lying in a manger." And suddenly there was with the angel a multitude of the heavenly host, praising God and saying, "Glory to God in the highest heaven, and on earth peace among those whom he favors." So the shepherds went with haste and found Mary and Joseph and the child lying in the manger.

Now invite each participant to prepare their symbol or picture. As they finish it, they can place it on the prayer table. Meanwhile, play or sing an appropriate Advent hymn, e.g., "Are We Ready for His Coming?" or "Patience, People."

MARY'S CANTICLE

Reader One	My soul magnifies the Lord, and my spirit rejoices in God my savior. For he has looked with favor on the lowliness of his servant. Surely from now on all generations will call me blessed.
All	My spirit rejoices in God my savior.
Reader Two	The Mighty One has done great things for me, and holy is his name. His mercy is on those who fear him from generation to generation.
All	My spirit rejoices in God my savior.
Reader Three	He has shown strength with his arm; he has scattered the proud in the thoughts of their hearts. He has brought down the powerful from their thrones, and lifted up the lowly.
All	My spirit rejoices in God my savior.
Reader Four	He has filled the hungry with good things, and sent the rich away empty. He has helped his servant Israel remembering his mercy.
All	My spirit rejoices in God my savior.
Reader Five	According to the promise he made to our ancestors, to Abraham and to his descendants forever.
All	My spirit rejoices in God my savior.

CLOSING PRAYER

Leader	Loving God, you sent us your greatest Gift in the person of your Son, Jesus Christ. Accept and bless our desire to practice the gifts of Advent, so as to keep the fire of love burning in our hearts. We ask all this through Jesus Christ your Son.
All	Amen.

Ask the participants to take their symbols with them as a reminder of the gifts of Advent.

Celebrating the Christmas Season

THEME

We rejoice together at the coming of Christ in history, in mystery, and in glory at the final coming.

PREPARATION

On the prayer table place a poinsettia plant or some holly and a small nativity scene. Play Christmas instrumental music as background during the prayer service.

ENTHRONEMENT OF THE BIBLE

Have a procession to enthrone the Bible (open to Luke 2:1–14). Carry the Bible and a lighted Christmas candle and place them on the prayer table. The readings and prayers of this prayer service point out the three comings of Christ. Let us open our hearts to all three.

GATHERING PRAYER

Leader	O God, with the light of your Son, the word of truth, dispel the darkness of ignorance and prejudice, and bring the warmth of love. We ask all this in Jesus' name.
All	Amen.

FIRST READING   Isaiah 62

Divide those gathered into two groups, each of which will alternate verses, as shown here.

All	Today is born our Savior, Christ the Lord.
Group One	We shall be a crown of beauty in your hand, O Lord, And a royal diadem in your hand, O God.
Group Two	We shall no more be termed Forsaken, And our land shall no more be termed Desolate;
Group One	But you, Lord shall call us "My Delight," And our land "married."
Group Two	For you, O Lord, delight in us And our land shall be married. For as a young man marries a young woman, So shall you, Lord, marry your people,
Group One	And as the bridegroom rejoices over his bride, so you, O God, shall rejoice over your people.
All	Today is born our Savior, Christ the Lord.

RESPONSORIAL PRAYER

Reader One	We praise you, Lord, with the lyre;
	Make melody to you with the harp of ten strings.
	Sing to you a new song.
All	All your faithful ones rejoice in you, Lord.
Reader Two	You love righteousness and justice;
	The earth is full of your steadfast love.
All	All your faithful ones rejoice in you, Lord.
Reader Three	By your word, O Lord, the heavens were made,
	And all their host by the breath of your mouth.
	Our soul waits for you, Lord; our heart is glad in you,
	Because we trust in your holy name.
All	All your faithful ones rejoice in you, Lord.

GOSPEL READING   Luke 2:1, 4–7

Reader One	In those days a decree went out from Emperor Augustus that all the world should be registered. Joseph also went from the town of Nazareth in Galilee to Judea, to the city of David called Bethlehem, because he was descended from the house and family of David. He went to be registered with Mary, to whom he was engaged and who was expecting a child. When they were there, the time came for her to deliver her child. And she gave birth to her firstborn son and wrapped him in bands of cloth, and laid him in a manger, because there was no place for them in the inn.
All	Praise to you, Lord Jesus Christ.

INTERCESSORY PRAYER

All	Christ our Lord became like us in all things. Let us praise him and say: Through your birth bring comfort to your people.
Reader Two	Once you were born as a poor little child.
All	Give hope to the poor and oppressed.
Reader Three	You brought the joy of everlasting life into the world.
All	Give joy to all your people, especially those who are suffering.
Reader Four	You came to bring good news to the people of all ages.
All	Be good news for us, the children we teach, and our families.

CLOSING PRAYER

Leader	Loving God, on this special feast we welcome Christ as our redeemer. As we rejoice in his presence, may we rejoice in his peace. We ask this in Jesus' name.
All	Amen.

You might want to close this prayer service by singing together a Christmas song.

We Offer Our Gifts (Epiphany)

THEME

In this ritual prayer service we offer symbolic gifts together with those of the magi, in response to the epiphany of Christ. This is the day of the amazing revelation of Christ and the kingdom of God.

PREPARATION

Prepare a table with the Bible (open to Matthew 2:1–12), a large white candle, and a crèche or large picture of the nativity. Ask each person to bring a symbol of the gifts and talents they bring to their catechetical ministry (e.g., a flower for joy, incense for prayer, a heart for love, and so on).

GATHERING PRAYER

Leader	Christ has come to dwell among us.
All	O come, let us adore him.

FIRST READING   2 Timothy 1:9–10

Reader One	God saved us and called us with a holy calling, not according to our works but according to his own purpose and grace. This grace was given to us in Christ Jesus before the ages began, but it has now been revealed through the appearing of our Savior Jesus Christ, who abolished death and brought life and immortality to light through the gospel.
All	Together with the magi we say, Come, let us worship the Lord.

LITANY

Reader Two	Arise, for God's light has come; your glory, O Lord, has risen upon us.
Reader Three	For darkness shall cover the earth, and thick darkness the peoples; but you, Lord, will rise upon us, and your glory will appear over us.
Reader Four	Nations shall come to your light, O Lord, and kings to the brightness of your dawn.
Reader One	Lift up your eyes, O people, and look around; your people all gather together, O Lord; they come to you.
Reader Two	The sun shall no longer be our light by day, nor shall the moon give us light by night; but you, Lord, will be our everlasting light, and you, God, will be our glory.

GOSPEL READING   Matthew 2:1–12

Reader Three	In the time of King Herod, after Jesus was born in Bethlehem of Judea, wise men from the East came to Jerusalem, asking, "Where is the child who has been born king of the Jews? For we have observed his star at its

	rising, and have come to pay him homage." Herod sent them to Bethlehem, saying, "Go and search diligently for the child, and when you have found him, bring me word so that I may also go and pay him homage." When they had heard the king, they set out; and there, ahead of them, went the star they had seen at its rising, until it stopped over the place where the child was.
All	Together with the magi we say, Come, let us worship the Lord.
Reader Four	When they saw that the star had stopped, they were overwhelmed with joy. On entering the house, they saw the child with Mary his mother, and they knelt down and paid him homage. Then, opening their treasure chests, they offered him gifts of gold, frankincense, and myrrh.
All	Together with the magi we say, Come, let us worship the Lord.

PRESENTATION OF THE GIFTS

Leader	Loving God, as the magi offered their gifts symbolizing Jesus' mission as king, priest, and prophet, we offer you symbols of the gifts we bring to our ministry as catechists. Bless these gifts and help us use them to give glory to your name, and to reveal your presence to the children we teach.

Invite those present to come up one by one to place their symbol on the prayer table, as you play or sing "We Three Kings."

INTERCESSORY PRAYER

Reader One	We have seen his star in the east and have come with gifts for the Lord.
All	We have come with gifts to worship you, Lord.
Reader Two	Lord, we pray for all our brothers and sisters around the world; may they be open to your gift of faith.
All	We have come with gifts to worship you, Lord.
Reader Three	Lord, as the magi placed their gifts at your feet, may we place our gifts at your service.
All	We have come with gifts to worship you, Lord.
Reader Four	Lord, we pray for the children we teach, who are very special gifts. May we help them grow closer to you.
All	We have come with gifts to worship you, Lord.

CLOSING PRAYER

Leader	God, our Creator, you led the wise men from the nations to your Son by the guidance of a star. Let the star of your love and wisdom help us follow him all the days of our lives. We ask this through your Son Jesus Christ.
All	Amen.

I Am Light, You Are Light

THEME

We are called to be light in the world, especially for those to whom we minister.

PREPARATION

Prepare a table with a Bible, a standing cross or crucifix, tapers, and a lenten wreath (a wreath made of dried vines or supple twigs, such as the kind found in craft stores), with six purple candles inserted into it, and with a large candle in the center. Give a taper to each person reading a prayer petition. Darken the room and light the large candle. Play reflective music.

GATHERING PRAYER

Leader	Loving God, you sent your Son to bring light into the darkness of the world. May we see everything in our lives in the light of our faith in Jesus, and help one another walk in that light. We ask this in Jesus' name.
All	Amen.

FIRST READING   Ephesians 5:8–14

Reader One	Once you were darkness, but now in the Lord you are light. Live as children of light—for the fruit of the light is found in all that is good and right and true. Try to find out what is pleasing to the Lord. Take no part in the unfruitful works of darkness, but instead expose them. Everything exposed by the light becomes visible, for everything that becomes visible is light.
All	May we live as children of light.

As each reader prays one of the following psalm verses, they light their taper from the large candle and then use it to light one of the candles on the lenten wreath.

RESPONSORIAL PRAYER

Reader Two	Lord, you are my light and my salvation; whom shall I fear? You are the stronghold of my life; of whom shall I be afraid?
All	Jesus, you are our light.
Reader Three	Though an army encamp against me, my heart shall not fear; though war rise up against me, yet I shall be confident.
All	Jesus, you are our light.
Reader Four	One thing I ask of you, Lord, that I will seek after: to live in your house, Lord, all the days of my life.
All	Jesus, you are our light.

Reader One	For you will hide me in your shelter in the day of trouble; you will conceal me in the cover of your tent; you will set me high on a rock.
All	Jesus, you are our light.
Reader Two	Hear, O Lord, when I cry aloud, be gracious to me and answer me! Your face, O Lord, I seek. Do not hide your face from me.
All	Jesus, you are our light.
Reader Three	I believe that I shall see your goodness, Lord, in the land of the living. Wait for the Lord; be strong and let your heart take courage; wait for the Lord!
All	Jesus, you are our light.

GOSPEL READING   John 9:1–7

Reader Four	As Jesus walked along, he saw a man blind from birth. His disciples asked him, "Rabbi, who sinned, this man or his parents, that he was born blind?" Jesus answered, "Neither this man nor his parents sinned; he was born blind so that God's works might be revealed in him. We must work the works of him who sent me while it is day; night is coming when no one can work. As long as I am in the world, I am the light of the world." When he had said this, he spat on the ground and made mud with the saliva and spread the mud on the man's eyes, saying to him, "Go, wash in the pool of Siloam." Then he went and washed and came back able to see.
All	Jesus, you are our light.

INTERCESSORY PRAYER

Reader One	Lord Jesus, you desire to lead us all to salvation. We implore you with all our hearts:
All	Lead us from darkness into the light.
Reader Two	Through the light of your word, open our minds and hearts to your truth,
All	May your word guide us in our choices and actions.
Reader Three	Grant that all who seek the truth, especially those whom we teach, may find it,
All	And in finding it, may they desire it even more.
Reader Four	May the light of your truth guide the decisions of all our leaders,
All	And bring us all to the peace we seek.

CLOSING PRAYER   *Join hands and pray:*

Leader	God of light, help us to be a light for others, as your Son Jesus calls us to be. We ask this in Jesus' name.
All	Amen.

Presentation of the Cross

THEME

This prayer ritual helps us celebrate one of the most powerful symbols of our faith.

PREPARATION

In this prayer service/ritual you will use oil to sign each participant with the sign of the cross and present them with a cross. Purchase or prepare inexpensive crosses or prayer cards with a cross on them, one for each participant. Prepare a table with a clear cruet of oil and a bowl in which to pour the oil. You may want to use oil with a slight color and pleasant scent. Place the crosses/prayer cards on the table, along with a Bible and a large cross or crucifix.

GATHERING PRAYER

Leader	Loving God, you call us to share a life of love and hope in Christ. May we treasure his cross as a sign of that new life. Help us be signs of Christ's love for one another and for the children and families we minister to. We ask this in Jesus' name.
All	Amen.

GOSPEL READING Matthew 16:24–27

Reader One	Then Jesus told his disciples, "If any want to become my followers, let them deny themselves and take up their cross and follow me. For those who want to save their life will lose it, and those who lose their life for my sake will find it. For what will it profit them if they gain the whole world but forfeit their life? Or what will they give in return for their life?"
All	Praise to you, Lord Jesus Christ.

RESPONSORIAL PRAYER

Reader Two	I call upon you, Lord; come to me quickly. Hear me when I call to you.
All	Lord, by your cross and resurrection you have set us free.
Reader Three	Let my prayer come like incense before you, and the lifting up of my hands like an evening sacrifice.
All	Lord, by your cross and resurrection you have set us free.
Reader Four	My eyes are turned to you, O Lord, my God; in you I seek refuge. Do not leave me defenseless.
All	Lord, by your cross and resurrection you have set us free.

From a sermon on the feast of the Holy Cross, by St. Andrew of Crete:

Reader One	We are celebrating the feast of the cross which drove away darkness and brought in the light. As we keep this feast, we are lifted up with the cruci-

fied Christ, leaving behind earth and sin so that we may gain the things above. Rightly could I call this treasure, the cross, the fairest of all fair things and the costliest, for on it and through it and for its sake the riches of salvation that had been lost were restored to us.

| All | We adore you, O Christ, and we bless you, for by your holy cross you have redeemed the world. |

PRESENTATION

Hold up the cruet of oil while praying:

| Leader | Lord, hear our prayer. Bless this oil, this fruit of the earth. Let it become your rich gift of strength and healing for your followers. |
| All | Amen. |

Pour the oil into the bowl. As you trace the sign of the cross on each forehead with the oil, say:

| Leader | (Name), I mark you with the sign of the cross. May it always remind you of God's love for you and the children you teach. |
| Each person responds | Amen. |

As you make the presentation of the crosses, say:

| Leader | You have been marked with the cross of Christ. Receive now the sign of his love. |
| Each person responds | Amen. |

INTERCESSORY PRAYER

Leader	Jesus, you bore the cross to save us all. Hear us as we pray:
All	We adore you, O Christ, and we bless you, for by your holy cross you have redeemed the world.
Reader Two	Jesus, though you were in the form of God, you emptied yourself to become one with us,
All	May we follow your example and not pride ourselves on our position.
Reader Three	Jesus, you were obedient to death and embraced your sufferings out of love,
All	May we imitate your obedience and acceptance of trials.
Reader Four	Jesus, at your name, every knee on heaven and earth should bow,
All	May we and those to whom we minister always honor your holy name.

CLOSING PRAYER

Based on a prayer of St. Patrick:

Christ be with me. Christ be beside me.
Christ be before me. Christ be behind me.
Christ be at my right hand. Christ be at my left hand.
Christ be with me everywhere I go.
Christ be my friend, forever and ever. Amen.

For Healing and Strength in Our Ministry

THEME

May reflection on the suffering Christ help us see his image in our children, as well as in the spiritually and materially needy in our world.

PREPARATION

On your prayer table place a Bible, a candle, and a crucifix, as well as pictures of children—photos, clippings from newspapers or magazines, etc.—mounted on a large piece of cardboard or a bulletin board and placed where all the participants can see them.

GATHERING PRAYER

Leader	Lord Jesus, may we be united in humility and charity, looking out for the interests of others—our colleagues, the children and families in our program—rather than our own. May we act not out of selfishness, or indifference, or convenience, but only out of love.
All	Amen.

FIRST READING Colossians 1:9–14

Reader One	Since the day we heard it, we have not ceased praying for you and asking that you may be filled with the knowledge of God's will in all spiritual wisdom and understanding, so that you may lead lives worthy of the Lord, fully pleasing to God, as you bear fruit in every good work and as you grow in the knowledge of God.
Reader Two	May you be made strong with all the strength that comes from God's glorious power, and may you be prepared to endure everything with patience, while joyfully giving thanks to the Father, who has enabled you to share in the inheritance of the saints in the light. God has rescued us from the power of darkness and transferred us into the kingdom of his beloved Son, in whom we have redemption, the forgiveness of our sins.
All	In Jesus we have redemption, the forgiveness of our sins.

RESPONSORIAL PRAYER

Reader Three	Lord God, you have given me the tongue of a teacher, that I may know how to sustain the weary with a word. Morning by morning you waken, waken my ear, to listen as those who are taught.

Reader One	Lord God, you have opened my ear, and I was not rebellious, I did not turn back. I gave my back to those who struck me, and my cheeks to those who pulled out my beard. I did not hide my face from insult and spitting.
Reader Two	You, O Lord, help me; therefore I have not been disgraced. I have set my face like flint, and I know that I shall not be put to shame.

GOSPEL READING   Luke 23:33–34, 39–43

Reader Three	When they came to the place that is called the Skull, they crucified Jesus there with the criminals, one on his right and one on his left. Then Jesus said, "Father, forgive them, for they do not know what they are doing." One of the criminals who were hanged there kept deriding him and saying, "Are you not the Messiah? Save yourself and us!" But the other rebuked him, saying, "Do you not fear God, since you are under the same sentence of condemnation? And we indeed have been condemned justly, for we are getting what we deserve for our deeds, but this man has done nothing wrong." Then he said, "Jesus, remember me when you come into your kingdom." Jesus replied, "Truly I tell you, today you will be with me in Paradise."

INTERCESSORY PRAYER

Reader One	For our weaknesses and failings, for our indifference and neglect, for our lack of faith, trust, and love in our ministry, we ask forgiveness.
All	We adore you, O Christ, and we praise you, because by your holy cross you have redeemed the world.
Reader Two	Let us soothe your hands and feet with deeds of loving service. Let us bathe your face and loosen the thorns on your head with thoughts of you and of those who may need our prayers and support.
All	We adore you, O Christ, and we praise you, because by your holy cross you have redeemed the world.
Reader Three	Let us lessen the pain of your pierced side with acts of love. May we be willing to risk—for you.
All	We adore you, O Christ, and we praise you, because by your holy cross you have redeemed the world.

CLOSING PRAYER

Leader	You know so well the children we teach, Lord. You know their thoughts and feelings, their dreams and hopes, their fears and discouragement, their joys and their sorrows. Surround them with your love and place your hand upon them. Grant us insight and sensitivity and respect for the mystery that each of them is—the mystery of a person made in your image. Help us to love them as you love them.
ALL	Amen.

Renewing Our Baptismal Promises

THEME
This prayer ritual is a reminder of our baptism and an opportunity to renew our baptismal commitment.

PREPARATION
On your prayer table place a Bible (open to John 15), a bowl with blessed water, a long clean piece of evergreen to use for the sprinkling, cards (preferably decorated) with the Renewal of Baptismal Promises on each, enough for each participant. (These promises appear below.) Play reflective background music.

GATHERING PRAYER

Leader	God our Father, by raising Christ your Son, you conquered the power of death and opened for us the way to eternal life. As we renew our baptismal promises, raise us up and renew our lives. We ask this in Jesus' name.
All	Amen.

FIRST READING   Ephesians 2:4–8

Reader One	God, who is rich in mercy, out of the great love with which he loved us even when we were dead through our trespasses, made us alive together with Christ—by grace you have been saved—and raised us up with him and seated us with him in the heavenly places in Christ Jesus, so that in the ages to come he might show the immeasurable riches of his grace in kindness toward us in Christ Jesus. For by grace you have been saved through faith, and this is not your own doing; it is the gift of God.
All	We have been saved through faith.

RESPONSORIAL PRAYER

Reader Two	I call upon you, for you will answer me, O God; incline your ear to me, hear my words.
All	Wondrously show your steadfast love.
Reader Three	Wondrously show your steadfast love, O savior of those who seek refuge from their adversaries at your right hand.
All	Wondrously show your steadfast love.
Reader Four	Guard me as the apple of your eye; hide me in the shadow of your wings, from the wicked who despoil me, my deadly enemies who surround me.

| All | Wondrously show your steadfast love. |

GOSPEL READING   John 15:1–5

| Reader Two | Jesus said to his disciples: "I am the true vine and my Father is the vine-grower. He removes every branch in me that bears no fruit. Every branch that bears fruit he prunes it to make more fruit. You have already been cleansed by the word that I have spoken to you. Abide in me as I abide in you. Just as the branch cannot bear fruit by itself unless it abides in the vine, neither can you unless you abide in me. I am the vine, you are the branches. Those who abide in me and I in them bear much fruit because apart from me you can do nothing." |
| All | I am the vine and you are the branches. |

RENEWAL OF BAPTISMAL PROMISES

After each question, all respond "I do."

Leader	Through the paschal mystery we have been buried with Christ in baptism so we may rise with him to newness of life. Now we will renew our baptismal promises as a sign of our commitment to Christ. Do you reject sin so you can live as God's children?
All	I do.
Leader	Do you refuse to be mastered by sin? *Response…*
Leader	Do you reject Satan? *Response…*
Leader	Do you believe in God who has created us? *Response…*
Leader	Do you believe in Jesus Christ who has redeemed us? *Response…*
Leader	Do you believe in the Holy Spirit who makes us holy? *Response…*

SPRINKLING RITE

Sing an appropriate hymn, such as "Water of Life," by Stephen Dean or "Flow, River, Flow," by Bob Hurd or play instrumental music as everyone is blessed with water.

INTERCESSORY PRAYER

Reader Three	Lord, our calling as ministers of the word comes from our baptism.
All	Help us to proclaim that word with love.
Reader Four	Lord, may we teach the children and families we minister to to always treasure the gift of their baptism,
All	And to make it bear fruit in their daily lives.

CLOSING PRAYER

| Leader | Through baptism into Christ's death we were buried with him. Just as Christ, who was raised from the dead by the glory of the Father, may we too live a new life. We ask this through Jesus Christ our Lord. |
| All | Amen. |

Developing a Vision

THEME

Vision means keeping our hearts and eyes and lives open to God's presence.

PREPARATION

On your prayer table place a Bible (open to Luke 24), a candle, and a loaf of freshly baked bread (not sliced), large enough for all the participants to have a small piece.

GATHERING PRAYER

Leader	Loving God, we gather in your presence to seek light and guidance in our ministry. Give us the courage to dream, the wisdom to realize our dreams, and the perseverance to bring them to completion.
All	Amen.

The readings in this prayer service point to ways of recognizing Christ in our daily lives.

FIRST READING	2 Peter 1:16–19
Reader One	We did not follow cleverly devised myths when we made known to you the power and coming of our Lord Jesus Christ, but we had been eyewitnesses of his majesty. For he received honor and glory from God the Father when that voice was conveyed to him by the Majestic Glory, saying, "This is my Son, my Beloved, with whom I am well pleased."
All	Keep your lamps burning brightly, until the morning star rises in your hearts.
Reader Two	We ourselves heard this voice come from heaven, while we were with him on the holy mountain. So we have the prophetic message more fully confirmed. You will do well to be attentive to this as to a lamp shining in a dark place, until the day dawns and the morning star rises in your hearts.
All	Keep your lamps burning brightly, until the morning star rises in your hearts.

RESPONSORIAL PRAYER

Reader Three	As a deer longs for flowing streams, so my soul longs for you, O God.
All	My soul longs for you, O God.
Reader Four	My soul thirsts for you, O God, the living God, when shall I come and behold your face, O God?
All	My soul longs for you, O God.
Reader Three	My hope is in you, O God; for I shall again praise you, my help and my God.

All	My soul longs for you, O God.
Reader Four	By day you, Lord, command your steadfast love, and at night your song is with me, a prayer to you, the God of my life.
All	My soul longs for you, O God.

GOSPEL READING   Luke 24:28–32

| Reader Five | As they came near the village to which they were going, Jesus walked ahead as if he were going on. But they urged him strongly, saying, "Stay with us because it is almost evening and the day is nearly over." So he went in to stay with them. When he was at the table with them, he took bread, blessed and broke it, and gave it to them. Then their eyes were opened and they recognized him, and he vanished from their sight. They said to each other, "Were not our hearts burning within us while he was talking to us on the road, while he was opening the scriptures to us?" |
| All | Stay with us, Lord. |

INTERCESSORY PRAYER

Reader One	Lord Jesus, be with us as you were with the disciples on the road to Emmaus. Open our eyes to see you and our ears to hear your voice.
All	Stay with us, Lord.
Reader Two	Be with us as we celebrate your presence in the Eucharist and in one another. May our hearts burn bright with love for you and for the children and families we minister to.
All	Stay with us, Lord.
Reader Three	Show us how to proclaim you, our Way, Truth, and Life, in word and deed. May every person we encounter become aware of your presence in their lives.
All	Stay with us, Lord.
Reader Four	Give us wisdom and vision, Lord Jesus. Help us to always know you in the Scriptures and in the breaking of the bread.
All	Stay with us, Lord.

PRAYER OF BLESSING OVER THE BREAD

| Leader | Lord Jesus, our God, as you blessed the bread and shared it with the disciples at Emmaus, so now bless this bread (make the sign of the cross over the bread), a sign of your presence with us. Sanctify us who break this bread together; may we be eucharist for one another. Bless and sanctify each person we hold in our hearts, all your people who long for you, and those who do not know you. Bless us with your truth and life. |
| All | Amen. |

Pass the loaf around, inviting each participant to take a piece and eat it.

Celebration of the Creed

THEME

Our common proclamation of faith is a living tradition handed down through the ages.

PREPARATION

Prepare a table with a Bible (open to Matthew), a large candle, a copy of the Creed in large print (either the Apostles' or the Nicene), tapers, and smaller copies of the Creed, one for each participant.

GATHERING PRAYER

Leader	God, our creator, you have revealed yourself to us down through the ages through prophets and saints. Through the Church you continue to teach us your truth, even through your little ones. Today we ask you to strengthen our faith, the faith we share with the children and families we minister to. We ask this in Jesus' name.
All	Amen.

Light the large candle.

As St. Paul reminds us, we are called by baptism not only to live our faith but to share it.

FIRST READING	Romans 1:8–12
Reader One	First, I thank my God through Jesus Christ for all of you, because your faith is proclaimed throughout the world. For God, whom I serve with my spirit by announcing the gospel of his Son, is my witness that without ceasing I remember you always in my prayers, asking that by God's will I may somehow at last succeed in coming to you. For I am longing to see you so that I may share with you some spiritual gift to strengthen you—or rather so that we may be mutually encouraged by each other's faith, both yours and mine. The word of the Lord.
All	Thanks be to God.

RESPONSORIAL PRAYER

Reader Two	Vindicate me, Lord, for I have walked in my integrity, and I have trusted in the Lord without wavering.
All	The one who is righteous will live by faith.
Reader Three	Prove me, O Lord, and try me; test my heart and mind. For your steadfast love is before my eyes, and I walk in faithfulness to you.
All	The one who is righteous will live by faith.
Reader Four	O Lord, I love the house in which you dwell, and the place where your glory abides. Redeem me and be gracious to me. My foot stands on level

ground, in the great congregation I will bless the Lord.

All   The one who is righteous will live by faith.

GOSPEL READING   Matthew 7:24–27

Reader One   Everyone then who hears these words of mine and acts on them will be like a wise man who built his house on rock. The rain fell, the floods came, and the winds blew and beat on that house, but it did not fall, because it had been founded on rock. And everyone who hears these words of mine and does not act on them will be like a foolish man who built his house on sand. The rain fell, and the floods came, and the winds blew and beat against that house, and it fell—and great was its fall!

All   The wise person builds their house on rock.

PROFESSION OF FAITH

Invite each of the participants to come up to the prayer table and take a taper, and light it from the large candle. At the same time they should take a copy of the Creed. You may substitute the Apostles' Creed below with the Profession of Faith—Nicene Creed—used at Mass.

Leader   Let us profess our faith.

All   I believe in God, the Father Almighty, creator of heaven and earth, and in Jesus Christ his only Son, our Lord, who was conceived by the Holy Spirit, born of the Virgin Mary, was crucified, died and was buried. He descended into hell; on the third day he rose again from the dead and ascended into heaven. He sits at the right hand of God, the Father Almighty; from there he shall come to judge the living and the dead. I believe in the Holy Spirit, the holy Catholic Church, the communion of saints, the forgiveness of sins, the resurrection of the dead, and life everlasting. Amen.

Extinguish candles.

INTERCESSORY PRAYER

Reader Two   Lord, look kindly on us who have renewed our profession of faith in you.

All   Lord, look kindly on your church.

Reader Three   Strengthen all who hope in you, especially those suffering in mind and body.

All   Lord, look kindly on your church.

Reader Four   Direct our feet in the ways of justice and peace, and lead those we minister to to follow in your footsteps.

All   Lord, look kindly on your church.

CLOSING PRAYER

Leader   Loving God, may we always be firm in our faith, courageous and strong. May we do everything out of love. We ask through Jesus Christ, your Son.

All   Amen.

Lord, Send Forth Your Spirit

THEME

Celebrating the Spirit's action in our ministry can lead to spiritual growth and greater openness to creativity.

PREPARATION

On your prayer table place a Bible (open to John 15), a large candle (red, if possible), and a collage of pictures symbolizing the action of the Spirit in our lives and our world (e.g., people helping one another, peace symbols, flames, nature scenes, etc.).

GATHERING PRAYER

Leader	Loving God, you have marked us with the seal of your Holy Spirit and have sent us out as disciples of your Son. Help us be temples of the Spirit and let us all give glory to your name. We ask this through Jesus, your Son.
All	Amen.

As we begin our prayer service, let us keep in mind the words from Galatians: "If we live by the Spirit, let us be guided by the Spirit."

FIRST READING Galatians 5:22—6:2

Reader One	The fruit of the Spirit is love, joy, peace, patience, kindness, generosity, faithfulness, gentleness, and self–control. There is no law against such things. And those who belong to Christ Jesus have crucified the flesh with its passions and desires. If we live by the Spirit, let us also be guided by the Spirit. Let us not become conceited, competing against one another, envying one another. Bear one another's burdens, and in this way you will fulfill the law of Christ.
All	If we live by the Spirit, let us be guided by the Spirit.

RESPONSORIAL PRAYER

Reader Two	Bless the Lord, O my soul. O Lord my God, you are very great. You are clothed with honor and majesty, wrapped in light as in a garment.
All	When you send forth your Spirit, you renew the face of the earth.
Reader Three	You set the earth on its foundations, so that it shall never be shaken. You cover it with the deep as with a garment; the waters stood above the mountains.
All	When you send forth your Spirit, you renew the face of the earth.
Reader One	Lord, how manifold are your works! In wisdom you have made them all; the earth is full of your creatures.
All	When you send forth your Spirit, you renew the face of the earth.

Reader Two	They all look to you to give them their food in due season; when you give to them, they gather it up; when you open your hand, they are filled with good things.
All	When you send forth your Spirit, you renew the face of the earth.
Reader Three	May your glory, Lord, endure forever; may you rejoice in your works. I will sing to you, Lord, as long as I live. Bless the Lord!
All	When you send forth your Spirit, you renew the face of the earth.

GOSPEL READING   John 15:26–27; 16:12–14

Reader Four	Jesus said to his disciples: "When the Advocate comes, whom I will send to you from the Father, the Spirit of truth who comes from the Father, he will testify on my behalf. You also are to testify because you have been with me from the beginning.... I still have many things to say to you, but you cannot bear them now. When the Spirit of truth comes, he will guide you into all the truth; for he will not speak on his own, but will speak whatever he hears, and he will declare to you the things that are to come. He will glorify me, because he will take what is mine and declare it to you." The gospel of the Lord.
All	Praise to you, Lord Jesus Christ.

Light the red candle. Stand around the prayer table and offer spontaneous prayers based on the collage. Then pray together the intercessory prayer.

INTERCESSORY PRAYER

Reader One	Spirit of God, give us your gifts of wisdom and knowledge,
All	Come, Holy Spirit.
Reader Two	Spirit of God, give us your gifts of understanding and counsel,
All	Come, Holy Spirit.
Reader Three	Spirit of God, give us your gifts of fortitude and piety,
All	Come, Holy Spirit.
Reader Four	Spirit of God, give us your gift of holy fear of the Lord,
All	Come, Holy Spirit.

CLOSING PRAYER

Leader	O God, you have instructed the hearts of the faithful by the light of your Holy Spirit. Grant that by that same Spirit we may judge what is truly right and ever rejoice in your consolation. Through Christ our Lord.
All	Amen.

Mary, Teacher and Disciple

THEME

Mary is both our teacher and the disciple of Jesus. We look to her example in our catechetical ministry.

PREPARATION

Gather around the prayer table on which you have placed the Bible (open to John 2:1–12), a candle, flowers, a picture or statue of Mary, and small cards, each with the outline of a large water jar, and the words "Do whatever he tells you" written inside the outline.

GATHERING PRAYER

Leader	Loving God, you chose Mary to be the mother of your Son, Jesus our Savior. Through her intercession, help us be faithful and loving disciples of Jesus. We ask this in Jesus' name.
All	Amen.

FIRST READING   Acts of the Apostles 1:12–14, 2:1–4

Reader One	After the ascension of Jesus, the disciples returned to Jerusalem from the mount called Olivet, which is near Jerusalem, a sabbath day's journey away. When they had entered the city, they went to the room upstairs where they were staying…including Mary the mother of Jesus, as well as his brothers.
	When the day of Pentecost had come, they were all together in one place. And suddenly from heaven there came a sound like the rush of a violent wind, and it filled the entire house where they were sitting. Divided tongues, as of fire, appeared among them, and a tongue rested on each of them. All of them were filled with the Holy Spirit.
All	Mary, stay with us.

RESPONSORIAL PRAYER

Adapted from the Book of the Wisdom of Solomon

Reader Two	Lord, your wisdom is a spirit that is intelligent, holy, unique, manifold, subtle, mobile, clear…loving the good, beneficent, humane, steadfast.
All	Hail, Mary, full of grace, pray for us.
Reader Three	Because of her pureness she pervades and penetrates all things. For she is a breath of your power, O God, and a pure emanation of your glory.
All	Hail, Mary, full of grace, pray for us.
Reader Four	Therefore nothing defiled gains entrance into her. For she is a reflection of your eternal light, Lord, a spotless mirror of your handiwork, and an

image of your goodness.

All   Hail, Mary, full of grace, pray for us.

GOSPEL READING   John 2:1–12

Reader Five   On the third day there was a wedding in Cana of Galilee, and the mother of Jesus was there. Jesus and his disciples had also been invited to the wedding. When the wine gave out, the mother of Jesus said to him, "They have no wine." And Jesus said to her, "Woman, what concern is that to you and to me? My hour has not yet come." His mother said to the servants, "Do whatever he tells you." Now standing there were six stone water jars for the Jewish rite of purification, each holding twenty or thirty gallons. Jesus said to them, "Fill the jars with water." And they filled them to the brim…. Jesus did this, the first of his signs, in Cana of Galilee, and revealed his glory; and his disciples believed in him. The Word of the Lord.

All   Praise to you, Lord Jesus Christ.

MARY'S CANTICLE

Reader One   My soul magnifies you, O Lord, and my spirit rejoices in you, my savior. You have looked with favor on the lowliness of your servant. Surely from now on all generations will call me blessed.

Reader Two   You, Mighty One, have done great things for me, and holy is your name. Your mercy is on those who fear you from generation to generation.

Reader Three   You have shown strength with your arm; you have scattered the proud in the thoughts of their hearts. You have brought down the powerful from their thrones, and lifted up the lowly.

Reader Four   You have filled the hungry with good things, and sent the rich away empty. You have helped your servant Israel, remembering your mercy.

Reader Five   According to the promise you made to our ancestors, to Abraham and to his descendants forever.

INTERCESSORY PRAYER

Reader One   Lord, you made Mary a teacher as well as a disciple of your Son.

All   Through her prayers may we share the gospel with the children and families we minister to.

Reader Two   Lord, you made Mary the pure temple of your Spirit.

All   Through her prayers may we grow in the gifts of the Spirit.

CLOSING PRAYER

Leader   Let us praise God for all his gifts, and ask Mary to join her prayers to ours.

All   Hail Mary….

Give each participant one of the prayer cards you prepared.

Jesus, Our Master Teacher

THEME

Jesus is the model for all catechists, and reading the Scriptures with faith helps us know him better. This prayer service uses the lectio divina method of praying the Scriptures.

PREPARATION

If necessary review the lectio divina method of praying the Scriptures (see Introduction).

ENTHRONEMENT OF THE BIBLE

Have a simple procession into the meeting space. One reader can carry a large candle, one can carry a picture of Jesus, and a third can carry the Bible. Each will place what they are carrying in the appropriate place on the prayer table.

GATHERING PRAYER

Leader	Loving God, you have given us your Son Jesus to be our Master Catechist: to be the Way that leads to you, the Truth that guides us, and the Life that fills us with joy. Help us listen to and follow Jesus, and learn from his way of teaching.
All	Amen.

FIRST READING From *The General Directory for Catechesis in Plain English* (Huebsch)

Reader One	Down through the ages, God has revealed himself to us, culminating in Christ, who completed and perfected Revelation. Jesus Christ is God's own Son, the final event among all the events of salvation history. Catechesis begins here: it must show who Jesus Christ is, his life and ministry, and present Christian faith as the following of Christ. Hence catechesis must be based on the gospels. In short, Christ is the center point of catechetical ministry (#40–41).

Take a few moments for silent reflection.

RESPONSORIAL PRAYER

Reader Two	Happy are those whose way is blameless, who walk in your law, Lord.
All	O God, you have made known to us the mystery of your will in Christ Jesus.
Reader Three	Happy are those who keep your decrees, who seek you with their whole heart, who also do no wrong, but walk in your ways.
All	O God, you have made known to us the mystery of your will in Christ Jesus.
Reader Four	With my whole heart I seek you; do not let me stray from your commandments. I treasure your word in my heart, so that I may not sin against

you. I delight in the way of your decrees as much as in all riches.

All   O God, you have made known to us the mystery of your will in Christ Jesus.

GOSPEL READING   John 11:17–27

Reader One   When Jesus arrived, he found that Lazarus had already been in the tomb four days. Now Bethany was near Jerusalem, some two miles away, and many of the Jews had come to Martha and Mary to console them about their brother. When Martha heard that Jesus was coming, she went out and met him, while Mary stayed at home. Martha said to Jesus, "Lord, if you had been here, my brother would not have died. But even now I know that God will give you whatever you ask of him."

Reader Two   Jesus said to her, "Your brother will rise again." Martha said to him, "I know that he will rise again in the resurrection on the last day." Jesus said to her, "I am the resurrection and the life. Those who believe in me, even though they die, will live, and everyone who lives and believes in me will never die. Do you believe this?" She said to him, "Yes, Lord, I believe that you are the Messiah, the Son of God, the one coming into the world."

Allow a few minutes of silence. Then invite whomever wishes to repeat aloud a sentence or phrase from the readings that struck her or him. Don't be afraid of silence—it allows you to reflect on the reading and is key to the meditative praying of the Scriptures. When everyone has shared who wishes to, invite all to silently reflect:

- What is this passage saying to me as a catechist, right now?
- How can I follow Christ the way, truth, and life concretely, daily, especially in my ministry to the children I teach?

Then allow time for spontaneous vocal prayer based on the reading and reflections.

CLOSING INTERCESSORY PRAYER

Reader Three   Jesus our Truth, increase our faith. Jesus our Way to the Father, may we follow in your footsteps. Jesus our Life, live in us so that we may live in you.

All   I am the Way, and the Truth, and the Life says the Lord. No one comes to the Father except through me.

Reader Four   Jesus, may we reflect your light for the children and families we minister to. May they hear you in our words and see you in our actions.

All   I am the Way, and the Truth, and the Life says the Lord. No one comes to the Father except through me.

Leader   Mary, mother and disciple, teach us how to listen to, follow, and love Jesus. Pray that we may be filled with the gifts of the Holy Spirit in our ministry and in our daily life.

All   Amen.

I Am with You

THEME

Catechesis is not just about doctrine; it's all about our relationship with God in Jesus Christ. Our catechetical ministry will be effective only if it is centered in the person of Christ. This prayer service uses the lectio divina method of praying the Scriptures.

PREPARATION

Prepare the prayer table with flowers, a large candle, and the Bible (open to John 14). Play reflective background music. Prepare tapers, enough for each person present. If necessary review the lectio divina method of praying the Scriptures (see Introduction).

GATHERING PRAYER

Leader	Loving God, nourish our minds with the knowledge of Jesus who is Way, Truth, and Life. Following his example, may we all grow in wisdom, grace, and virtue. We ask all this in Jesus' name.
All	Amen.

FIRST READING — Philippians 1:20–26

Reader One   It is my eager expectation and hope that I will not be put to shame in any way, but that by my speaking with all boldness, Christ will be exalted now as always in my body, whether by life or by death. For to me, living is Christ and dying is gain. If I am to live in the flesh, that means fruitful labor for me; and I do not know which I prefer. I am hard pressed between the two: my desire is to depart and be with Christ, for that is far better; but to remain in the flesh is more necessary for you. Since I am convinced of this, I know that I will remain and continue with all of you for your progress and joy in faith, so that I may share abundantly in your boasting in Christ Jesus when I come to you again.

Light the large candle.

GOSPEL READING — John 14:1–6

Reader Two   Jesus said to his disciples: "Do not let your hearts be troubled. Believe in God, believe also in me. In my Father's house there are many dwelling places. If it were not so, would I have told you that I go to prepare a place for you? And if I go and prepare a place for you, I will come again and will take you to myself, so that where I am, there you may be also. And you know the way to the place where I am going." Thomas said to him, "Lord, we do not know where you are going. How can we know the way?" Jesus said to him, "I am the way, and the truth, and the life. No one comes to the Father except through me."

Allow a few minutes of silence. Then invite whomever wishes to repeat aloud a sentence or phrase from the readings that struck her or him. Don't be afraid of silence—it allows you to reflect on the reading and is key to the meditative praying of the Scriptures. When everyone has shared who wishes to, invite all to silently reflect:

- What is this passage saying to me as a catechist, right now?
- How can I follow Christ the way, truth, and life concretely, daily, especially in my ministry to the children I teach?

Then allow time for spontaneous vocal prayer based on the reading and reflections.

LITANY

Reader Three	You, O Lord, say: I am at the root and origin of your existence.
All	Lord, I believe in you.
Reader Four	I am the dawn without end.
All	Lord, I believe in you.
Reader Five	I am the present without a past.
All	Lord, I believe in you.
Reader One	I am your life in the Eucharist.
All	Lord, I believe in you.
Reader Two	I am your Savior and your God.
All	Lord, I believe in you.

REFLECTION PRAYER

Reader Three	"I am with you…." How many times have we all heard these or similar words? How many times others have said them to us, family or friends, to let us know that they are there for us and that they care for us?
Reader Four	But when you, Lord, say, "I am with you," the words are infinitely more powerful. When you take our hand, when you look into our eyes…when you send us a sunrise or rainbow…when you show us your cross…you say, "I am with you."
Reader Five	Your "I am with you," means so much because it enables us to say yes when you ask us to choose you as the center of our lives.

Allow a few moments of silence.

CLOSING PRAYER

Leader	Stay with us, Lord Jesus, and with those we teach. Be our strength and inspiration in our catechetical ministry. Help us keep our lives centered in you. We ask all this through the intercession of your mother Mary.
All	Amen.

Love as I Love You

THEME

Life is God loving us into existence—and each of us loving one another into existence. This prayer service uses the lectio divina method of praying the Scriptures.

PREPARATION

Prepare a table with a vase of flowers, one flower for each participant. Gather around the table. If necessary review the lectio divina method of praying the Scriptures (see Introduction). Play reflective music.

ENTHRONEMENT OF THE BIBLE

Have a simple procession into the meeting space. One reader can carry a large candle and the other will carry the Bible. Each will place what they are carrying in the appropriate place on the prayer table. Gather around the table.

GATHERING PRAYER

Leader	God of goodness and compassion, we thank and praise you for your steadfast love. You satisfy our thirst and fill the hungry with good things. Into the dry desert of human failings bring the living waters of your grace. We ask this through your Son Jesus.
All	Amen.

FIRST READING	Isaiah 43:1–5a
Reader One	But now you say, O Lord, you who created Jacob, you who formed Israel: "Do not fear for I have redeemed you; I have called you by name, you are mine." You tell us: "When you pass through the waters, I will be with you; and through the rivers they shall not overwhelm you: when you walk through the fire you shall not be burned, and the flame shall not consume you." You are the Lord our God, the Holy One of Israel, our Savior. You say to us: "You are precious in my sight, and honored, and I love you. Do not fear for I am with you."

Allow a few minutes of silence. Then invite whomever wishes to repeat aloud a sentence or phrase from the readings that struck her or him. Don't be afraid of silence—it allows you to reflect on the reading and is key to the meditative praying of the Scriptures. When everyone has shared who wishes to, invite all to silently reflect:

- What is this passage saying to me as a catechist, right now?
- How can I follow Christ the way, truth, and life concretely, daily, especially in my ministry to the children I teach?

Then allow time for spontaneous vocal prayer based on the reading and reflections.

RESPONSORIAL PRAYER

Reader Two	We will sing forever of your steadfast love, O Lord.
All	We will sing forever of your steadfast love, O Lord.
Reader Three	We will proclaim your faithfulness to every generation. Your steadfast love is established forever; your faithfulness is as firm as the heavens.
All	We will sing forever of your steadfast love, O Lord.
Reader Four	You said, "I have made a covenant with my chosen one." Let the heavens praise your wonders, O Lord. For who can compare to you, O Lord?
All	We will sing forever of your steadfast love, O Lord.
Reader One	Even when we are unfaithful, when we do not follow your law, you do not cease to love us. You are forever faithful.
All	We will sing forever of your steadfast love, O Lord.

GOSPEL READING   John 15:12–17

Reader Two	Jesus said to his disciples: "This is my commandment, that you love one another as I have loved you. No one has greater love than this, to lay down one's life for one's friends. You are my friends if you do what I command you. I do not call you servants any longer, because the servant does not know what the master is doing, but I have called you friends, because I have made known to you everything that I have heard from my Father. You did not choose me but I chose you. And I appointed you to go and bear fruit, fruit that will last, so that the Father will give you whatever you ask him in my name. I am giving you these commands so that you may love one another."

Again allow a few minutes of silence and follow the steps for sharing as above.

CLOSING PRAYER

Reader Three	This is my commandment, that you love one another as I have loved you.
All	This is my commandment, that you love one another as I have loved you.
Reader Four	No one has greater love than this, to lay down one's life for one's friends.
All	This is my commandment, that you love one another as I have loved you.
Reader One	I call you friends because I have made known to you everything that I have heard from my Father.
All	This is my commandment, that you love one another as I have loved you.
Reader Two	Loving God, you have formed each of us in your image. Give us the love and wisdom to seek the best solutions to situations and conditions that threaten human dignity and the sacredness of human life, and to put our resolves into practice. We ask this in Jesus' name.
All	Amen.

Invite each of the participants to take one of the flowers from the vase and keep it as a reminder to be bearers of God's love.

Where Your Treasure Is

THEME

As ministers of the word, this word of God must be a treasure we delight in sharing. This prayer service uses the lectio divina method of praying the Scriptures.

PREPARATION

You will need a table with a small, decorated "treasure" box containing slips of paper, each with one or two symbols of Catholic beliefs and practices and of important aspects of your parish faith formation program. If possible, provide a copy of the Bible for each participant, or type and photocopy today's passage, Matthew 13:44–53. Play reflective instrumental music. If necessary, review the lectio divina method of praying the Scriptures (see Introduction).

Before the gathering prayer, ask everyone to think about what the treasures are in their lives right now.

GATHERING PRAYER

Leader	Spirit of Love, open our minds and hearts to God's word. By listening to and living this word may we be a light to others, as Jesus is our light. We ask this in Jesus' name.
All	Amen.

GOSPEL READING Matthew 13:44–46, 51–52

Reader One	Jesus said: "The kingdom of heaven is like treasure hidden in a field, which someone found and hid; then in his joy he goes and sells all that he has and buys that field. Again the kingdom of heaven is like a merchant in search of fine pearls; on finding one pearl of great value, he went and sold all he had and bought it. Have you understood all this?" They answered, "Yes." And Jesus said to them, "Therefore every scribe who has been trained for the kingdom of heaven is like the master of a household who brings out of his treasure what is new and what is old."

Allow a few minutes of silence. Then invite whomever wishes to repeat aloud a sentence or phrase from the readings that struck her or him. Don't be afraid of silence—it allows you to reflect on the reading and is key to the meditative praying of the Scriptures. When everyone has shared who wishes to, invite all to silently reflect:

- What is this passage saying to me as a catechist, right now?
- How can I follow Christ the way, truth, and life concretely, daily, especially in my ministry to the children I teach?

Then allow time for spontaneous vocal prayer based on the reading and reflections.

RESPONSORIAL PRAYER

Reader Two	We rejoice in you, Lord. We praise you with the melody of our lives. We sing a new song to you. For your word is truth and all that you do shows your faithfulness. You love integrity and justice. The earth is full of your steadfast love.
All	Lord, we entrust ourselves to you.
Reader Three	Your counsel, Lord, stands forever, the thoughts of your heart are known to all generations. Happy is the nation whose God you are, the people whom you have chosen as your heritage.
All	Lord, we entrust ourselves to you.
Reader Four	Our whole being waits for you, Lord; you are our help and protector. Our hearts are glad in you, because we trust in your holy name. Let your steadfast love be with us, Lord, as we hope in you.
All	Glory to the Father, and to the Son, and to the Holy Spirit, forever and ever. Amen.

We thank God for the treasure of his word with Mary's song of praise.

MARY'S CANTICLE

Reader One	My soul magnifies you, O Lord, and my spirit rejoices in you, my savior. You have looked with favor on the lowliness of your servant. Surely from now on all generations will call me blessed.
Reader Two	You, Mighty One, have done great things for me, and holy is your name. Your mercy is on those who fear you from generation to generation. You have shown strength with your arm; you have scattered the proud in the thoughts of their hearts.
Reader Three	You have brought down the powerful from their thrones, and lifted up the lowly. You have filled the hungry with good things, and sent the rich away empty. You have helped your servant Israel, remembering your mercy.
Reader Four	According to the promise you made to our ancestors, to Abraham and to his descendants forever. Glory to the Father and to the Son and to the Holy Spirit, as it was in the beginning, is now, and will be forever. Amen.

Then open the "treasure box." Tell the participants that these symbols represent treasures of your faith and of your parish life. Invite each person to take one of the "treasures" in the treasure box. Encourage them to keep it in a visible place as a reminder of their faith.

CLOSING PRAYER

Leader	Loving God, your word is our treasure. May it guide our every thought and action. Help us to share your word with one another and with the children you have entrusted to us in our catechetical ministry. We ask this in the name of Jesus your Son.
ALL	Amen.

For Wisdom in Our Ministry

THEME

One of the gifts of the Spirit, wisdom, is certainly important in a catechist's ministry.

PREPARATION

On your prayer table place a Bible (open to Matthew 13); a candle; packets of seeds; and lists of the children in each religion class if possible typed or printed out on decorated stationery.

GATHERING PRAYER

Leader	Loving God, you have called each of us to serve you and your people in the catechetical ministry. Give us wisdom to guide and instruct the children and families entrusted to us. Lead us in your truth and teach us, for you are the God of our salvation, and we look to you all day long.
All	Amen.

FIRST READING 1 Corinthians 2:1–7, 12

Reader One	When I came to you, brothers and sisters, I did not come proclaiming the mystery of God to you in lofty words or wisdom. For I decided to know nothing among you except Jesus Christ and him crucified. And I came to you in weakness and fear and much trembling. My speech and my proclamation were not with plausible words of wisdom, but with a demonstration of the Spirit and of power, so that your faith might rest not on human wisdom but on the power of God.
All	May we know nothing but Jesus Christ.
Reader Two	Yet among the mature we do speak wisdom, though it is not a wisdom of this age or of the rulers of this age, who are doomed to perish. But we speak God's wisdom, secret and hidden which God decreed before the ages for our glory.... Now we have received, not the spirit of the world but the Spirit that is from God, so that we may understand the gifts bestowed on us by God.
All	May we know nothing but Jesus Christ.

RESPONSORIAL PRAYER

Reader Three	Both we and our words are in your hands, O God, as are all understanding and skill in crafts. We have learned both what is secret and what is manifest, for wisdom, the fashioner of all things, taught us.
All	Spirit of wisdom, fill our hearts.
Reader Four	In every generation wisdom passes into holy souls and makes them your

friends, O God; for you love nothing so much as the person who lives with wisdom.

| All | Spirit of wisdom, fill our hearts. |

Before the following reading give each participant some seeds (preferably in a packet) to hold as they listen to the reading.

GOSPEL READING   Matthew 13:18–23

Reader One	Jesus said to his disciples: "Hear then the parable of the sower. When anyone hears the word of the kingdom and does not understand it, the evil one comes and snatches away what is sown in the heart; this is what was sown on the path. As for what was sown on rocky ground, this is the one who hears the word and immediately receives it with joy; yet such a person has no root but endures only for a while, and when trouble or persecution comes on account of the word, that person immediately falls away."
Reader Two	"As for what was sown among thorns, this is the one who hears the word but the cares of the world and the lure of wealth choke the word, and it yields nothing. But as for what was sown on good soil, this is the one who hears the word and understands it, who indeed bears fruit and yields, in one case a hundredfold, in another sixty, and in another thirty."
All	Jesus, may we be the good soil that yields a hundredfold.

INTERCESSORY PRAYER

Reader Three	Lord, may we nourish your word in our lives so it can bear fruit.
All	Sow your word in our hearts.
Reader Four	May we use every means to nurture the word in the lives of those to whom we minister.
All	Sow your word in our hearts.
Reader One	May we sow the seed lavishly, with faith that you will give it abundant growth.
All	Sow your word in our hearts.
Leader	Take these seeds home and plant them as a reminder of our need to grow in wisdom.

CLOSING PRAYER

| Leader | God of our Lord Jesus Christ, Father of glory, give us a spirit of wisdom and revelation as we come to know you. Enlighten the eyes of our hearts so that we may know the hope to which you have called us, the riches of your glorious inheritance among the saints, and the immeasurable greatness of your power for all of us who believe. |
| All | Amen. |

Invite the participants to take the list of the children in their class with them and place it somewhere to remind them to pray for those they teach.

Celebrating Reconciliation

THEME

Reconciliation is an important gift in our daily life. In this service we ask to live that gift. This prayer service uses the lectio divina method of praying the Scriptures.

PREPARATION

Prepare a table with a Bible (open to Luke 15); a candle; a large metal bowl, charcoal, incense, and matches. Hand out slips of paper to all the participants. If necessary review the lectio divina method of praying the Scriptures (see Introduction).

Before beginning the prayer service, let us all think of someone with whom we need to be reconciled.

GATHERING PRAYER

Leader	Loving God, you forgive us even before we ask. Open our hearts and minds to the gift of reconciliation. Teach us how to forgive and to ask forgiveness, and how to model reconciliation for those we teach.
All	Amen.

FIRST READING   Colossians 3:12–17

Reader One	As God's chosen ones, holy and beloved, clothe yourselves with compassion, kindness, humility, meekness, and patience. Bear with one another and, if anyone has a complaint against another, forgive each other; just as the Lord has forgiven you, so you also must forgive. Above all, clothe yourselves with love, which binds everything together in perfect harmony.
All	Forgive one another as the Lord has forgiven you.

RESPONSORIAL PRAYER

Reader Two	Incline your ear, O Lord, and answer me, for I am poor and needy. Preserve my life, for I am devoted to you; save your servant who trusts in you.
All	To you, O Lord, I lift up my soul.
Reader Three	You are my God; be gracious to me, O Lord; for to you I cry all day long. Gladden the soul of your servant, for to you, O Lord, I lift up my soul.
All	To you, O Lord, I lift up my soul.
Reader Four	For you, O Lord, are good and forgiving, abounding in steadfast love to all who call on you.
All	To you, O Lord, I lift up my soul.
Reader One	Teach me your way, O Lord, that I may walk in your truth; give me an undivided heart to revere your name.

All	To you, O Lord, I lift up my soul.
Reader Two	For you, O Lord, are a God merciful and gracious, slow to anger and abounding in steadfast love and faithfulness.
All	To you, O Lord, I lift up my soul.

GOSPEL READING   Luke 15:1–7

| Reader Three | Now all the tax collectors and sinners were coming near to listen to Jesus. And the Pharisees and scribes were grumbling and saying, "This fellow welcomes sinners and eats with them." So he told them this parable: "Which one of you, having a hundred sheep and losing one of them, does not leave the ninety–nine in the wilderness and go after the one that is lost until he finds it? When he has found it, he lays it on his shoulders and rejoices. And when he comes home, he calls together his friends and neighbors, saying to them, 'Rejoice with me, for I have found my sheep that was lost.' Just so, I tell you there will be more joy in heaven over one sinner who repents than over ninety–nine righteous persons who need no repentance." |
| All | Rejoice with me, for I have found my lost sheep. |

Allow a few minutes of silence. Then invite whomever wishes to repeat aloud a sentence or phrase from the readings that struck her or him. When everyone has shared who wishes to, invite all to silently reflect:

- What is this passage saying to me as a catechist, right now?
- How can I practice reconciliation concretely, daily, especially in my ministry to the children I teach?

Invite everyone to write on their slip of paper one particular area in which they feel the need to grow spiritually. Light the charcoal in the metal bowl, place the incense in, then the slips of paper, burning them as a symbol of prayer.

INTERCESSORY PRAYER

Reader One	Lord, look kindly on us who seek to cleanse our hearts and to be one with you and with our sisters and brothers.
All	Lord, grant us forgiveness and peace.
Reader Two	We pray for all children who are victims of injustice.
All	Lord, grant us forgiveness and peace.
Reader Three	We pray for all those whom society shuts out: the poor, the imprisoned, the mentally disabled. May we embrace them with love.
All	Lord, grant us forgiveness and peace.

CLOSING PRAYER

| Leader | Merciful God, we rejoice in your loving kindness, shown especially to us in your Son Jesus Christ. May we follow his example of mercy and forgiveness, and share that example with the children and families we minister to. |
| All | Amen. |

Beatitudes

THEME

In the beatitudes we find a guide to Christian living for all of us.

PREPARATION

On the prayer table place a Bible (open to Matthew 5), a large candle, and a large piece of poster paper. Ask each participant to bring in a contemporary picture of a person/people practicing one of the beatitudes. Assign eight readers and give each one a card with one of the beatitudes. Explain to all the participants that this will be a form of lectio divina. After each beatitude is read, there will be a few moments of silence. Any of the participants can briefly share their reflections on that beatitude. Then everyone who has brought a picture applicable to that beatitude can attach it to the sheet of poster paper.

GATHERING PRAYER

Leader	Loving God, open our hearts and minds as we listen to the beatitudes your Son proclaimed to his disciples of every age. Help us live according to those guidelines for happiness, following in Jesus' footsteps. We ask this in his name.
All	Amen.

FIRST READING   Philippians 2:12–16

Reader One	Therefore, my beloved, just as you have always obeyed me, not only in my presence, but much more now in my absence, work out your own salvation with fear and trembling; for it is God who is at work in you, enabling you both to will and to work for his good pleasure. Do all things without murmuring and arguing, so that you may be blameless and innocent, children of God without blemish in the midst of a crooked and perverse generation, in which you shine like stars in the world. It is by your holding fast to the word of life that I can boast on the day of Christ that I did not run or labor in vain.
All	Hold fast to the word of life.

LITANY OF THE BEATITUDES

Reader One	Blessed are the poor in spirit, for theirs is the kingdom of heaven.
All	Lord, may we be the salt of the earth.

Pause for reflection and sharing. Attach pictures to poster.

Reader Two	Blessed are those who mourn for they shall be comforted.
All	Lord, may we be the salt of the earth.

Pause for reflection and sharing. Attach pictures to poster.

| Reader Three | Blessed are the meek, for they will inherit the earth. |
| All | Lord, may we be the salt of the earth. |

Pause for reflection and sharing. Attach pictures to poster.

| Reader Four | Blessed are those who hunger and thirst for righteousness, for they will be filled. |
| All | Lord, may we be the salt of the earth. |

Pause for reflection and sharing. Attach pictures to poster.

| Reader One | Blessed are the merciful, for they will receive mercy. |
| All | Lord, may we be the salt of the earth. |

Pause for reflection and sharing. Attach pictures to poster.

| Reader Two | Blessed are the pure in heart, for they will see God. |
| All | Lord, may we be the salt of the earth. |

Pause for reflection and sharing. Attach pictures to poster.

| Reader Three | Blessed are the peacemakers, for they will be called children of God. |
| All | Lord, may we be the salt of the earth. |

Pause for reflection and sharing. Attach pictures to poster.

| Reader Four | Blessed are those who are persecuted for righteousness' sake, for theirs is the kingdom of heaven. |
| All | Lord, may we be the salt of the earth. |

Pause for reflection and sharing. Attach pictures to poster.

MARY'S CANTICLE

| All | My soul magnifies you, O Lord, and my spirit rejoices in you, my savior. You have looked with favor on the lowliness of your servant. Surely from now on all generations will call me blessed. You, Mighty One, have done great things for me, and holy is your name. Your mercy is on those who fear you from generation to generation. You have shown strength with your arm; you have scattered the proud in the thoughts of their hearts. You have brought down the powerful from their thrones, and lifted up the lowly. You have filled the hungry with good things, and sent the rich away empty. You have helped your servant Israel, remembering your mercy, according to the promise you made to our ancestors, to Abraham and to his descendants forever. |

CLOSING PRAYER

| Leader | Merciful God, you have called us to be the salt of the earth and the light of the world. May our words and actions witness to the blessedness of those who live your gospel. We ask this in Jesus' name. |
| All | Amen. |

Peace

THEME

Peace needs to be lived at all levels. In this prayer we ask for the deepest kind of peace that comes from God.

PREPARATION

On your prayer table place a Bible, a large candle, and incense. Play some soft reflective music. Have a small paper dove for each participant.

GATHERING PRAYER

Leader	Loving God, source of our peace, hear the prayers that come from our hearts. We offer you the works of our hands as a sign of our commitment to peace. Bless us and all those who strive for peace in our world.
All	Amen.

This lovely image from Isaiah reminds us that peace is possible.

FIRST READING	Isaiah 11:6–9
Reader One	The wolf shall live with the lamb, the leopard shall lie down with the kid, the calf and the lion and the fatling together, and a little child shall lead them. The cow and the bear shall graze, their young shall lie down together; and the lion shall eat straw like the ox. They will not hurt or destroy on my holy mountain; for the earth will be full of the knowledge of the Lord as the waters cover the sea. The word of the Lord.
All	Thanks be to God.

RESPONSORIAL PRAYER

Reader Two	I bless you, Lord, with all that is within me. Blessed is your holy name.
All	Bless the Lord, O my soul.
Reader Three	I bless you Lord, and I do not forget all your benefits—how you forgive all our iniquity, how you heal all our diseases.
All	Bless the Lord, O my soul.
Reader Four	For you crown us with steadfast love and mercy, you satisfy us with good as long as we live, so that our youth is renewed like the eagle's.
All	Bless the Lord, O my soul.
Reader One	Lord, you are merciful and gracious, slow to anger and abounding in steadfast love. As a father has compassion for his children, so you, Lord, have compassion for those who fear you.
All	Bless the Lord, O my soul.

GOSPEL READING	John 20:19–23
Reader Two	When it was evening on that day, the first day of the week, and the doors of the house where the disciples had met were locked for fear of the Jews, Jesus came and stood among them and said, "Peace be with you." After he said this, he showed them his hands and his side. Then the disciples rejoiced when they saw the Lord. Jesus said to them again, "Peace be with you. As the Father has sent me, so I send you." When he had said this, he breathed on them and said to them, "Receive the Holy Spirit. If you forgive the sins of any, they are forgiven them; if you retain the sins of any, they are retained."

SPONTANEOUS SHARING

Give each participant one of the paper doves. Invite each of them to write a petition for peace on it. Then ask the participants to spontaneously and prayerfully share with the group what they have written or drawn, and why or how it signifies peace to them.

After each person shares, have everyone pray: Lord, grant us peace. This response should be followed by a few moments of silence so that each participant can reflect on what has been said.

If time permits, put some pieces of charcoal (the kind used for burning incense in church) in a large metal bowl. Light the charcoal; when it has burned for a few moments, add the incense as a sign of your prayers rising to God. When there is a good glow, invite each person, one by one, to fold their sheet of paper and place it in the bowl as an offering to God.

As you are carrying out this ritual, say the "Peace Prayer of St. Francis."

Lord, make me a channel of your peace.
Where there is hatred, let me sow love,
Where there is injury, pardon.
Where there is doubt, faith.
Where there is despair, hope.
Where there is darkness, light.
And where there is sadness, joy.

O Divine Master, grant that I may not seek
so much to be consoled, as to console,
to be understood as to understand,
to be loved as to love.
For it is in giving that we receive,
It is in pardoning that we are pardoned,
And it is in dying that we are born to eternal life.

The Bread of Life

Note: You will need access to an oven for this activity.

THEME
This special prayer ritual involves participants in making bread as a symbol of oneness and life. The theme is thanksgiving: for Jesus the bread of life and for one another, as we are the bread of life for each other.

PREPARATION
Gather the ingredients for making a loaf of bread:

2 cups whole wheat flour
1 cup white flour
4 teaspoons baking powder
1 teaspoon salt

1/2 cup shortening
1 and 1/3 cups milk
3 tablespoons honey

Place the ingredients on your prayer table, along with a large mixing bowl, a large spoon, a spatula, and a wooden board covered with flour (for kneading the bread). If your group is large, you may want to have two sets of ingredients, bowls, etc., on two separate tables. Assign some participants to be readers and others to add the ingredients to the bowl. Pair each reader with the correct ingredient. Ask both readers and "cooks" to make the bread prayerfully, and to add each ingredient after the appropriate blessing is said.

GATHERING PRAYER

Leader	Loving God, you nourish us with all good things, so that we might care for one another. As we prepare this bread of thanksgiving, let our hearts be open to your love. We ask this in Jesus' name.
All	Amen.

GOSPEL READING   John 6:35–40

Reader One	Jesus said to them, "I am the bread of life. Whoever comes to me will never be hungry, and whoever believes in me will never be thirsty. Everyone who has heard and learns from the Father comes to me. I am the living bread that came down from heaven. Whoever eats of this bread will live forever; and the bread that I will give is my flesh." This is the gospel of the Lord.
All	Praise to you, Lord Jesus Christ.

RESPONSORIAL PRAYER

Reader Two	For as the rain and the snow come down from heaven, and do not return

	there until they have watered the earth.
All	Your word, Lord, nourishes the earth.
Reader Three	Making it bring forth and sprout, giving seed to the sower and bread to the eater, so shall my word be that goes out from my mouth; it shall not return to me empty but shall accomplish my purpose.
All	Your word, Lord, nourishes the earth.
Reader Four	For you shall go out in joy, and be led back in peace; the mountains and the hills before you shall burst into song, and all the trees of the field shall clap their hands.
All	Your word, Lord, nourishes the earth.

MAKING THE BREAD

Reader One	Lord, bless this flour, used to make bread which is a staple of life. Help each of us be committed to the faith formation of the children and families we minister to. (Pour the flour into the bowl.)
Reader Two	Loving God, bless this leaven, which causes the loaf to rise. Jesus has compared leaven to the kingdom of God. Help each of us to be an influence for good in the lives we touch. (Pour the baking powder into the bowl and mix it with the flour.)
Reader Three	Lord, bless this salt, which seasons and preserves food. Jesus has called each of us to be the salt of the earth. May we keep our own faith strong and active, so as to be better catechists. (Pour the salt into the bowl and mix it.)
Reader Four	Loving God, bless this shortening (or oil) which moistens and makes the dough smooth. May we be the oil that helps, comforts, and strengthens those to whom we minister. (Add the shortening to the mix and stir until it is blended.)
Reader One	Lord, bless this milk which nourishes us from the moment we are born. We thank you for the privilege of helping nurture others with your word. (Pour in the milk and blend it in.)
Reader Two	Loving God, bless this honey which sweetens our food and our lives. Help us be kind, understanding, and caring ministers of your gospel. (Pour the honey into the bowl and blend everything together.)
Reader Three	Lord, bless all these ingredients and the bread they make. Jesus the bread of life calls each of us to break bread together and to be the bread of life for others. (Knead the dough, form it into a loaf, place it onto the floured board, and make certain both sides are covered with flour.)
Reader Four	Bless us all, Lord, and help us support one another. Only together, following your son Jesus, can we accomplish our mission as catechists. We ask this through Jesus your Son.
All	Amen.

After the prayer service, have someone finish preparing the dough and bake it. Bread is baked in a 375° oven for about 45 minutes. Share it later on with the participants.

We Are Called to Nurture Life

THEME

As catechists we must be in the forefront of respect for and defense of life.

PREPARATION

Prepare the prayer table with flowers, a Bible (open to Matthew 11), and a large candle. Invite participants to each bring a symbol of or information about something he or she can do to nurture life, to place on the prayer table during the prayer service. Ask everyone to hold in their hearts all those whose innocent lives are threatened in our society.

GATHERING PRAYER

Leader	Lord Jesus, may we always heed your invitation: "Come to me, all you who are weary and find life burdensome, and I will refresh you. Take my yoke upon your shoulders and learn from me, for I am gentle and humble of heart. Your souls will find rest" (Mt 11:28–29). We pray for all those whose innocent lives are threatened. Hear us, Jesus, through the intercession of your mother.
All	Amen.

GOSPEL READING Luke 13:10–17

Reader One	Jesus was teaching in one of the synagogues on the Sabbath. Just then there appeared a woman with a spirit that had crippled her for eighteen years. She was bent over and was quite unable to stand up straight. When Jesus saw her, he called her over and said, "Woman, you are set free from your ailment." When he laid his hands on her, immediately she stood up straight and began praising God. But the leader of the synagogue, indignant because Jesus had cured on the Sabbath, kept saying to the crowd, "There are six days on which work ought to be done; come on those days to be cured, and not on the Sabbath day." But the Lord answered and said, "You hypocrites! Does not each of you on the Sabbath untie his ox or his donkey from the manger and lead it away to give it water? And ought not this woman, a daughter of Abraham...be set free from this bondage on the Sabbath day?" When he said this, all his opponents were put to shame; and the entire crowd was rejoicing at all the wonderful things that he was doing.
All	Praise to you, Lord Jesus!

RESPONSORIAL PRAYER

Form participants into two groups, and have them pray alternating verses.

Group One	In you, O Lord, every person finds refuge; may we, too, be a refuge to those in need, and never put a sister or brother to shame.
Group Two	May we hear their cry and in your name assist them and deliver them.
Group One	May we help those who fall into the hands of persons who would do them harm. May we protect them from the grasp of the violent.
Group Two	You are our hope, O God, our trust, O God, from our youth. On you we depend from the moment of our birth; you are our strength and the giver of life from the moment we are conceived.
Group One	May we cherish your gift, and be a sign to many, especially to our children and families, of the dignity of the human person.
Group Two	May we not cast aside the elderly, or those whose strength fails them, those who are ill or disabled, those who are defenseless, those who need our compassion.
Group One	May we keep watch and speak out against those who threaten the life of a sister or brother. May we nurture the life of each person you have created, and may we teach others to do the same.
All	Glory be to the Father....

PRESENTATION OF SYMBOLS

As the following prayers and responses are read, each person or group of people can bring their symbols and place them in the prepared area.

Leader	We thank you, Lord, for the precious gift of life, our own and that of every person. Help us to care for this gift and use it for the good of others.
All	Lord, help us nurture life.
Leader	Lord, touch the hearts of those who do not respect the gift of life.
All	Lord, help us nurture life.
Leader	Lord, help us do all we can to lessen and remove the evils of abortion, euthanasia, the death penalty, war, drugs, discrimination, and more.
All	Lord, help us nurture life.
Leader	Enlighten the minds and move the hearts of our government leaders; may they bring about an order that promotes, protects, and values the gift of life.
All	Lord, help us nurture life.
Leader	May our parish be a community of believers grounded in faith, motivated by compassion, and empowered by the Spirit to reach out to others.
All	Lord, help us nurture life.

CLOSING PRAYER

Leader	Loving God, help us always to walk in the light as you are the light. May our belief in the value of life shine in everything we do and say. We ask this in Jesus' name.
All	Amen.

Called to Promote Justice

THEME

An important part of our mission is to teach children and adults about social justice and the Church's teaching. You can use the ritual fast to raise your own awareness of justice issues. This prayer service uses the lectio divina method of praying the Scriptures.

PREPARATION

Decide together on a day when you can all fast for at least half the day, reflect on your experience, and then meet for prayer. In your meeting place, lay a Bible on a cushion in the middle of the room and kneel in a circle around it. If possible light one or two large candles. Bring some seeds in a bowl, a coin, and a symbol of corporate or personal greed. If necessary, review the lectio divina method of praying the Scriptures (see Introduction).

GATHERING PRAYER

Leader	God of love and justice, your care reaches from end to end of our world and orders all things in such a way that even the tensions and effects of sin cannot alter your loving plans. Give us all the courage to change the things we can and the wisdom to know the difference.
All	Amen.

FIRST READING — Amos 7:4, 6, 7

Reader One	Hear this, you that trample on the needy, and bring ruin to the poor of the land, buying the poor for silver, and the needy for a pair of sandals. The Lord has sworn by the pride of Jacob; surely I will never forget any of their deeds.
All	I am the refuge of the poor.

Allow a few minutes of silence. Then invite whomever wishes to repeat aloud a sentence or phrase from the readings that struck her or him. When everyone has shared who wishes to, invite all to silently reflect:

- What is this passage saying to me as a catechist, right now?
- How can I promote justice, especially in my ministry to the children I teach?

RESPONSORIAL PRAYER

Pass around the bowl of seeds.

Reader Two	Hear this, you that trample on the needy, and bring to ruin the poor of the land, saying, "When will the new moon be over so we may sell grain?"
All	I the Lord will not forget injustice.

Pass around the coin.

Reader Three	We will make the ephah small and the shekel great, and practice deceit with false balances.
All	I the Lord will not forget injustice.

Pass around the contemporary symbol.

Reader Four	Surely I will never forget any of these deeds, says the Lord. I will turn your feasts into mourning and your songs into lamentation.
All	I the Lord will not forget injustice.

GOSPEL READING Matthew 25:31–40

Reader One	Jesus said: "When the Son of Man comes in his glory, all the people will be gathered, some on his right and some on his left. To those on his right he will say, 'Come, blessed of my Father, inherit the kingdom prepared for you, for I was hungry and thirsty and naked and a stranger and imprisoned, and you cared for me in my need.' And those on his right will ask, 'When did we do this, Lord?' And he will answer, 'Whenever you did this for one of my brothers and sisters, you did it for me.'"

Allow a few moments. Follow the same sharing process as above.

INTERCESSORY PRAYER

Reader Two	Lord, the work for justice in any age can seem overwhelming. The sea looks so big, and our boat looks so small. Help us have faith that we can make a difference, however big or small, in our world, by changing one thing at a time, beginning with ourselves.
Reader Three	Lord, may our attitude toward the poor be one of compassion and not judgment. We pray:
All	Lord, hear our prayer
Reader Four	Lord, may we have the courage to take practical steps to right what is wrong in our neighborhood and our nation. We pray:
All	Lord, hear our prayer
Reader One	Lord, may we support organizations who uphold the rights of the poor and the oppressed, who seek to reverse injustices, even on the corporate level. We pray:
All	Lord, hear our prayer
Reader Two	Lord, we know that by ourselves we can accomplish nothing. Multiply and bless the efforts of all who work for the cause of justice. We ask this through Jesus your Son. Amen.

CLOSING PRAYER

Sing or pray the Our Father.

St. Paul, an Example of Living in Christ

THEME

As catechists we can take inspiration from the apostle Paul. Let this prayer service also be an incentive to read and study the letters of St. Paul.

PREPARATION

On your prayer table place a red candle and, if possible, a picture of St. Paul (found in books that feature lives of the saints or on the Internet).

ENTHRONEMENT OF THE BIBLE

Have a simple procession into the meeting space. One reader can carry a large candle, another can carry the Bible. Each will place what they are carrying in the appropriate place on the prayer table.

GATHERING PRAYER

Leader	God of wisdom and love, in your apostle Paul you have given us the example of a disciple filled with zeal for your word. May we be as dedicated to our ministry of catechesis as he was to his, in the footsteps of Jesus. We ask all this in Jesus' name.
All	Amen.

FIRST READING

1 Corinthians 9:16–23

Reader One	If I proclaim the gospel, this gives me no ground for boasting, for an obligation is laid on me, and woe to me if I do not proclaim the gospel! For if I do this of my own will, I have a reward; but if not of my own will, I am entrusted with a commission. What then is my reward? Just this: that in my proclamation I may make the gospel free of charge, so as not to make full use of my rights in the gospel.... I have become all things to all people, that I might by all means save some. I do it all for the sake of the gospel, so that I may share in its blessings. The word of the Lord.
All	Thanks be to God.

RESPONSORIAL PRAYER

Leader	The following prayers are taken from the letters of St. Paul, asking for various virtues needed by a minister of the word. Pause in silence for a few moments after each prayer.
Reader Two	To know and live the will of God, Lord, fill us with the knowledge of your

	will in all spiritual wisdom and understanding, so that we may lead lives worthy of you, be fully pleasing to you, bearing fruit in every good work and growing in the knowledge of God (Col 1:9–10). *Pause.*
All	May the grace of our Lord Jesus Christ be with us.
Reader Three	To ask for holiness of life…God of peace, sanctify us entirely; and may our spirit and soul and body be kept sound and blameless at the coming of our Lord Jesus Christ. You call us, and you are faithful (1 Thes 5:23). *Pause.*
All	May the grace of our Lord Jesus Christ be with us.
Reader Four	To ask for love for God and for one another…Lord, make us increase and abound in love for one another and for all. Strengthen our hearts in holiness that we may be blameless before you at the coming of our Lord Jesus with all his saints (1 Thes 3:12–13). *Pause.*
All	May the grace of our Lord Jesus Christ be with us.
Reader One	To ask for a spirit of wisdom…God of our Lord Jesus Christ, the Father of glory, give us a spirit of wisdom and revelation as we come to know you, so that, with the eyes of our hearts enlightened, we may know what is the hope to which you have called us (Eph 1:17–18). *Pause.*
All	May the grace of our Lord Jesus Christ be with us.
Reader Two	To proclaim the gospel…Since it is by God's mercy that we are engaged in this ministry, may we not lose heart. For we do not proclaim ourselves, we proclaim Jesus Christ as Lord, and ourselves as servants for Jesus' sake. We have this treasure in clay jars so that it may be made clear that this extraordinary power belongs to God and does not come from us (2 Cor 4:1, 5, 7). *Pause.*
All	May the grace of our Lord Jesus Christ be with us.

GOSPEL READING Matthew 10:5–13

Reader Three	Jesus sent the twelve with the following instructions: "Go and proclaim the good news. The kingdom of heaven has come near. Cure the sick, raise the dead, cleanse the lepers, cast out demons. You received without payment, give without payment. Whatever town or village you enter, find out who in it is worthy, and stay there until you leave. As you enter the house, greet it. If the house is worthy let your peace come upon it; but if it is not worthy, let your peace return to you."
All	The kingdom of heaven is near.

CLOSING PRAYER

Leader	God who said, "Let the light shine in the darkness," has shone in our hearts, in order to radiate the knowledge of the divine glory that glows on the face of Christ. Through the prayers of the apostle Paul may we reflect that glory to others, especially those we teach through our ministry.
All	Amen.

Canticle of the Media

THEME

We thank the Lord for the means he places at our disposal for sharing his word. How many ways do you know how to incorporate media into your sessions?

PREPARATION

On your prayer table prepare a Bible (open to Matthew 10), flowers, and a collection of pictures representing TV, videos, radio, computer games, and so on.

GATHERING PRAYER

Leader	We bless you, Lord, for all the forms of media used to present Christian values in various ways. May we use these same media effectively in our ministry of catechesis. We pray for this in the name of Jesus, your Son.
All	Amen.

FIRST READING — From the *General Directory for Catechesis in Plain English* (Huebsch)

Reader One	Well-planned catechetical programs must use all the modern media available to them in order to be more fully effective. In fact, it's more than merely bringing media into the classroom setting. It involves making a serious commitment to integrating the Christian message into the new culture of modern media, using new languages, new techniques, and a new psychology.... The media should help to make the gospel present by animating a passion for the truth, working in defense of liberty, respecting the dignity of all, and elevating the culture of peoples. (#160–162)

RESPONSORIAL PRAYER

Reader Two	We praise you, Lord, from the heavens; we praise you in the heights! All your angels praise you! All your heavenly host praise you!
All	We praise you, Lord, from the heavens.
Reader Three	The sun and moon praise you, Lord; all your shining stars praise you! Your highest heavens praise you, and the waters above the heavens.
All	We praise you, Lord, from the heavens.
Reader Four	We praise your name, O Lord, for you commanded and we were created. You established us forever and ever.
All	We praise you, Lord, from the heavens.

GOSPEL READING — Matthew 10:40—11:6

Reader One	Jesus said to his disciples: "Whoever welcomes you welcomes me, and

whoever welcomes me, welcomes the one who sent me. Whoever welcomes a prophet in the name of a prophet will receive a prophet's reward. Whoever welcomes a just person in the name of a just person will receive the reward of a just person. Whoever gives even a cup of cold water to one of these little ones in the name of a disciple—truly I tell you, none of these will lose their reward.

When John heard in prison what the Messiah was doing, he sent word by his disciples and said to him, "Are you the one who is to come, or are we to wait for another?" Jesus answered them, "Go and tell John what you hear and see: the blind receive their sight, the lame walk, the lepers are cleansed, the deaf hear, the dead are raised, and the poor have the good news brought to them."

CANTICLE OF THE MEDIA

Reader Two	Praise to you, Lord, for the gift of film, which can bring answers for important questions to a large audience.
All	Praise to you, Lord, for the media.
Reader Three	Praise to you, Lord, for the gift of television, which can bring the good news into thousands of homes.
All	Praise to you, Lord, for the media.
Reader Four	Praise to you, Lord, for the gift of CDs, which we can use to praise God with music.
All	Praise to you, Lord, for the media.
Reader Five	Praise to you, Lord, for the radio, which we can use to communicate the word even outside the home.
All	Praise to you, Lord, for the media.
Reader One	Praise to you, Lord, for the gift of good computer games, which we can use to involve children in learning.
All	Praise to you, Lord, for the media.
Reader Two	Praise to you, Lord, for the gift of the printed word, which makes the word of God visible for all to read.
All	Praise to you, Lord, for the media.

CLOSING PRAYER

Leader	Loving God, you bless us with so many wondrous gifts, including the inventions of technology that come from the intelligence and creativity you have bestowed on men and women. May we always use these gifts for your glory and the good of all people.
All	Amen.

OPTION: You could take some time to brainstorm with your catechetical team and write your own "canticle of the media," blessing the Lord for each form of media and for those involved in creating them. Then use your canticle as the closing prayer.

Holy Friendship

THEME

Supportive friendships can help us perform our ministry with more sensitivity. This prayer service uses the lectio divina method of praying the Scriptures.

PREPARATION

Obtain some 3" x 5" index cards (one for each participant). On each write one of the positive qualities of friendship from Sirach (see below). On your prayer table place a Bible (open to Ephesians 4), a candle, and the index cards. Play reflective background music. If necessary review the lectio divina method of praying the Scriptures.

GATHERING PRAYER

Leader	God our Father, we give you thanks that we are wonderfully made. May we love and respect one another as images of you and temples of your Spirit. May we be true friends to one another and wise companions to the children and families we minister to. We ask all this through Jesus your Son.
All	Amen.

Invite a few of the participants to pantomime these images from the first reading—shelter, treasure, medicine, friend—as the reading is slowly proclaimed.

FIRST READING	Sirach 6:14–17
Reader One	Faithful friends are a sturdy shelter; whoever finds one has found a treasure. Faithful friends are beyond price; no amount can balance their worth. Faithful friends are like life-saving medicine; and those who fear the Lord will find them. Those who fear the Lord direct their friendship aright, for as they are, so are their neighbors also.
All	Faithful friends are beyond price.

Allow a few minutes of silence. Then invite whomever wishes to repeat aloud a sentence or phrase from the reading that struck her or him. Don't be afraid of silence—it allows you to reflect on the reading and is key to the meditative praying of the Scriptures. When everyone has shared who wishes to, invite all to silently reflect:

- What is this passage saying to me as a catechist, right now?
- What does friendship mean to me right now in my personal life? In my ministry?

RESPONSORIAL PRAYER

Reader Two	Lord, let us hear what you will speak, for you will speak peace to your people, to your faithful, to those who turn to you in your hearts.
Reader Three	Surely your salvation is at hand for those who fear you, that your glory may dwell in our land.

| Reader Four | Steadfast love and faithfulness will meet; righteousness and peace will kiss. Faithfulness will spring up from the ground and righteousness will look down from the sky. |

The letter to the Ephesians also describes what is needed for a holy friendship.

SECOND READING Ephesians 4:22–24, 31—5:2

| Reader Five | Put away your former way of life, your old self, and be renewed in the spirit of your minds. Clothe yourselves with the new self, created according to the likeness of God in true righteousness and holiness. Put away from you all bitterness and wrath and anger and wrangling and slander, together with all malice, and be kind to one another, tenderhearted, forgiving one another, as God in Christ has forgiven you. Therefore be imitators of God, as beloved children, and live in love, as Christ loved us and gave himself up for us. |
| All | May we live in love as Christ loved us. |

Allow a few moments of silence. Follow the same steps for sharing.

INTERCESSORY PRAYER

Reader One	Friendships bring great joy and enrichment to the lives of many people. Let us pray for supportive friends who can help us perform our ministry with more sensitivity.
Reader Two	Lord, bless all friends near and far. Especially bless our family members, who are often our best and truest friends.
All	Faithful friends are a treasure.
Reader Three	May we be the kind of friend described in Sirach: "a sturdy shelter…lifesaving medicine…."
All	Faithful friends are a treasure.
Reader Four	Lord, may we teach our children how to be good friends to one another: respectful, kind, forgiving one another.
All	Faithful friends are a treasure.

CLOSING PRAYER

| Leader | Loving God, may our love overflow more and more with knowledge and full insight—especially for the children entrusted to us—so that on the day of Christ we may be pure and blameless, having produced the harvest of holiness that comes through Jesus Christ for the glory and praise of God. We ask this in Jesus' name. |
| All | Amen. |

Invite each participant to take an index card and carry it with them throughout the day as a reminder of the vocation to love.

The Gift of Love

THEME
Love is a great gift that can transform our own lives and those of everyone with whom we come in contact. This prayer service uses the lectio divina method of praying the Scriptures.

PREPARATION
On your prayer table place a Bible (open to Matthew 22); a candle; pictures and photos from newspapers or magazines that show selfless love in action, enough for one picture for each participant. Provide a copy of the Bible for each participant; or type and photocopy today's passage from 1 Corinthians. If necessary, review the lectio divina method.

ENTHRONEMENT OF THE BIBLE
Have a simple procession into the meeting space. One reader can carry a large candle, another can carry the Bible. Each will place what they are carrying in the appropriate place on the prayer table. Play reflective instrumental background music. Gather around the table and light the candle.

GATHERING PRAYER

Leader	Loving God, you give your gifts of grace for every time and season as you guide us in the marvelous ways of your love. Send your Spirit to open our minds and hearts to that love and show us how to live it in our catechetical ministry. We ask this through your Son Jesus.
All	Amen.

FIRST READING   1 Corinthians 13:1–8

Reader One	If I speak in the tongues of mortals and of angels, but do not have love, I am a noisy gong or a clanging cymbal. And if I have prophetic powers, and understand all mysteries and all knowledge, and if I have all faith, so as to remove mountains, but do not have love, I am nothing. If I give away all my possessions, and if I hand over my body so that I may boast, but do not have love, I gain nothing. Love is patient; love is kind; love is not envious or boastful or arrogant or rude. It does not insist on its own way; it is not irritable or resentful; it does not rejoice in wrongdoing but rejoices in the truth. It bears all things, believes all things, hopes all things, endures all things. Love never ends. The word of the Lord.
All	Thanks be to God.

RESPONSORIAL PRAYER

Reader Two	When Israel was a child, I loved him, and out of Egypt I called my son.
All	Lord, your love carries us faithfully.

Reader Three	It was I who taught Ephraim to walk, I took them up in my arms; but they did not know that I healed them.
All	Lord, your love carries us faithfully.
Reader Four	I led them with cords of human kindness, with bands of love. I was to them like those who lift infants to their cheeks. I bent down to them and fed them.
All	Lord, your love carries us faithfully.

GOSPEL READING   Matthew 22:34–40

| Reader Five | When the Pharisees heard that Jesus had silenced the Sadducees, they gathered together, and one of them, a lawyer, asked him a question to test him. "Teacher, which commandment in the law is the greatest?" He said to him, "'You shall love the Lord your God with all your heart, and with all your soul, and with all your mind.' This is the greatest and first commandment. And a second is like it: 'You shall love your neighbor as yourself.' On these two commandments rest all the law and the prophets." |

Allow a few minutes of silence. Then invite whomever wishes to repeat aloud a sentence or phrase from the reading that struck her or him. When everyone has shared who wishes to, invite all to silently reflect:

- What is this passage saying to me as a catechist, right now?

- How can I live the gift of love concretely, especially in my ministry to the children I teach?

INTERCESSORY PRAYER

Reader One	May our love extend to everyone, and not be limited by preferences or prejudice, we pray to the Lord,
All	Lord, hear our prayer.
Reader Two	May our love show itself in compassion toward those who are more needy, we pray to the Lord,
All	Lord, hear our prayer.
Reader Three	May our love be filled with understanding for the weakness of others, as well as our own, we pray to the Lord,
All	Lord, hear our prayer.
Reader Four	May our love for the children and families in our program help lead them closer to Jesus,
All	Lord, hear our prayer.

CLOSING PRAYER

| Leader | Spirit of love, in every age you raise up holy men and women to show us how to love God and one another. Help us learn from the example of the saints how to live the gift of love, and be examples of love to one another and to the children and families we minister to. |
| All | Amen. |

Of Related Interest

How to Be a Great DRE
Six Steps for Catechetical Leaders
Gail Thomas McKenna

This experienced DRE shares her ideas and encouragement with those who are striving to provide the best for their parish faith formation program. These six steps include discerning, calling forth, empowering, sharing a vision, reaching out, and nourishing oneself. She offers concrete suggestions, sample forms, organizational tools and more.   1-58595-229-X, 96 pp, $14.95

How to Be a Great Catechist
Judene Leon Coon

In this "how-to" book Judene Coon, an experienced religious educator, shares some sound advice on such topics as making the best use of time, connecting catechesis with liturgy, using pictures in religion class, how to ask the right questions, teaching prayer, issues of discipline, making use of the internet, and much more. What makes this book unique is that Judene offers not just theory but concrete examples of easy-to-do activities to illustrate her suggestions. An invaluable handbook for anyone involved in faith formation.
1-58595-274-5, 168 pp, $12.95

A Teacher's Prayerbook
To Know and Love Your Students
Ginger Farry

Prayer poems for and about students are followed by brief reflections or questions for teachers to ponder in relation to their own students.   0-89622-727-8, 64 pp, $4.95

I Like Being in Parish Ministry
Catechist
Alison Berger

Alison Berger invites catechists to probe the heart of their vocation: to help those they minister to know, celebrate, live, and contemplate the mystery of Christ and so grow in communion with him. With stories, reflection questions, and concrete suggestions, she guides us in exploring the spiritual and practical dimensions of catechizing as Jesus did.   1-58595-214-1, 48 pp, $4.95

I Like Being in Parish Ministry
Catechical Leader: DRE and CRE
Christopher Anderson

Catechetical leaders at all levels perform a crucial and multi-task ministry. Here, Chris Anderson reflects on the history and role of catechetical leadership in the Church, and highlights the qualities needed to successfuly fulfill this demanding vocation.   1-58595-215-X, 48 pp, $4.95

TWENTY-THIRD PUBLICATIONS
185 WILLOW STREET • PO BOX 180 • MYSTIC, CT 06355
TEL: 1-800-321-0411 • FAX: 1-800-572-0788
Bayard   E-MAIL: ttpubs@aol.com • www.twentythirdpublications.com